Cities are exciting places, but they can also be noisy, crowded, polluted, dangerous, and unattractive. Suburbs offer fresh air, greenery, and more spacious living quarters, but they lack an economic mix and are dependent on larger cities for jobs and social activities. Can young people growing up today hope for a better living alternative in the future? They may be able to find it in New Towns. These complete communities built from scratch are an attempt to combine the best of the city with the best of the country.

Martha Munzer and John Vogel skillfully trace the New Town movement from its beginnings in England to the first incomplete American New Town built in the 1920s, the government New Towns of the 1930s, and the rebirth of the New Town movement in the sixties and seventies. They show how each New Town borrowed ideas from previous New Towns, but also made its own important innovations. The authors also discuss the exciting possibilities for the future—including a floating city and a city covered with a dome.

# NEW TOWNS

# NEW TOWNS
## BUILDING CITIES FROM SCRATCH
by MARTHA E. MUNZER
and JOHN VOGEL, JR.

ALFRED A. KNOPF ✦ NEW YORK

Grateful acknowledgment is made for use of the following illustrations:

New York Public Library Picture Collection, 11, 130; Commission for the New Towns, Welwyn, England, 41; *Long Island Press*, 53; Trumble and Associates Inc., Minneapolis, Minn., 58, 115, 118; John H. Mitchell, Massachusetts Audubon Society, 76; The Rouse Company, 98; The Rouse Company, Photo by Jerry Wachter, Baltimore, Md., 103; Cedar-Riverside Associates, Inc., 122, 125; Walt Disney World Co., © Walt Disney Productions, 133.

THIS IS A BORZOI BOOK PUBLISHED BY ALFRED A. KNOPF, INC.

Copyright © 1974 by Martha Munzer and John Vogel, Jr. All rights reserved under International and Pan-American Copyright Conventions. Published in the United States by Alfred A. Knopf, Inc., New York, and simultaneously in Canada by Random House of Canada Limited, Toronto. Distributed by Random House, Inc., New York. Manufactured in the United States of America.

*Library of Congress Cataloging in Publication Data*

Munzer, Martha E. New towns: building cities from scratch. *Summary:* Profiles the founder of the "New Town" movement and discusses the development of British new towns, the Radburn Idea, Greenbelt Towns, and the American new towns such as Reston and Columbia. 1. Cities and towns—Planning—Juvenile literature. [1. Cities and towns—Planning. 2. Howard, Sir Ebenezer, 1850–1928] I. Vogel, John, joint author. II. Title. HT166.M84 309.2′62 74-158 ISBN 0-394-92673-0 (lib. bdg.) 0 9 8 7 6 5 4 3 2 1

To John and Helen Vogel, for today,
To David and Isaac Mosgrove, for tomorrow.

# Acknowledgments

The writing and publication of this book were made possible through the generous assistance of a great many people.

First there is Robert Simon, Jr. whose course on New Towns at the New School for Social Research helped to familiarize us with the field.

Then comes Professor Charles S. Ascher, International Representative of the Institute of Public Administration, whose lifelong involvement and wide acquaintance with the New Town movement opened many doors for us, both in this country and in Great Britain.

Among our British hosts we wish to give special thanks to Mr. and Mrs. Arthur Lamb of Letchworth; Sir Frederic Osborn; Mr. F. J. Harris and Mrs. Edith Meyer of Welwyn Garden City; and our gracious guides at Stevenage and Basildon. We are also indebted to Mr. Frank Schaffer, Secretary of the Commission for the New Towns, who was kind enough to confer with us before we left England, and who subsequently read and criticized our chapters on the British New Towns.

When we returned home, Mr. Jack Underhill of the U.S. Department of Housing and Urban Development was most helpful in discussing with us the present role of the federal government in support of New Communities.

Warm thanks go to Mr. Ronald Gatti, Manager of the Radburn Association; Mr. and Mrs. Vernon Walker of Reston's Nature Center; Mr. Owen Williams, on the legal staff of the Rouse Company; Mr. William R. Bone, Assistant Vice President of Marketing of the Rouse Company; Mr. Julius Smith, Senior Vice President and General Counsel for the Jonathan Development Corporation; and Mr. Robert Kneppers, of the Department of Planning and Development of Cedar-Riverside Associates.

To the other acquaintances made on our visits to the various New Towns our appreciation for their kindness and helpfulness. Some of these people are introduced by name in the course of our story. Others are omitted because there just wasn't room. To all we offer our general but nonetheless genuine thanks.

We wish also to acknowledge our indebtedness to Brown Miller, Neil Pinney and William Saslow. We first conceived the idea of writing a chapter on new technologies as related to New Towns from their book *Innovation in New Communities*. Some of the material we used was gleaned from this study.

A special thank you goes to Craig Stenberg, who was our host when we visited in Minnesota, and who shared many of our bull sessions in the course of our work.

An oft-repeated word of appreciation goes to Dr. Nancy Ziebur for her painstaking and perceptive suggestions on the complete text. And an added thank you to Dr. Ascher for his useful criticisms of the entire manuscript.

For her efficient and patient work in the many typings and retypings of the manuscript, we owe our thanks to Mrs. John Secco.

A final word of gratitude to our editors, Fabio Coen and Liz Phillips, without whose tireless and creative partnership our book could never have been put between covers.

# Contents

# NEW TOWNS

Chapter **1**   **The Human Settlement: Its Life Cycle**

Do you live in an urban setting? The chances are that you do, for today most of us in the United States live in the cities or their offshoots, the suburbs.

Central cities can be exciting places. They are magnets that attract us because they offer richness and variety in things to do, in sights to see, in people to rub shoulders with, and most importantly, in jobs to find. Better than any book, they tell the history of our people and their aspirations, in elaborately decorated cathedrals or sleek, functional, modern skyscrapers.

But cities can also be frightening places: the noise, the confusion of traffic jams, the pall of smog, the want of greenery, the lack of safety, especially after dark. And there are subtler drawbacks: the higher cost of living, the feeling of being lost and engulfed amidst huge buildings, and the impersonality of often being surrounded by strangers. Something has gone wrong. What a far cry is the typical city of today from the one envisioned by the ancient Greek philosopher Aristotle, who declared: "Men come together in cities to live; they remain there in order to live the good life."

1

What has happened? Where did we go wrong? For answers, let us review briefly the life cycle of a typical American city.

In colonial days, a settlement sprang up in a favorable location, safe from attack yet with easy access to the world beyond its borders. Church, school, village hall, homes, and workshops were clustered around a village green.

When the inhabitants began to feel crowded and hemmed in, the most adventuresome set out for greener pastures. These pioneers erected a new meeting house, enclosed a new common, laid out fresh fields for farming, built themselves new homes, and created a new village or town.

But, as our colonies grew, this pattern of settlement changed. Transportation improved, commerce and industry expanded, and more and more people crowded into these towns. The simple plans of an earlier day gave way to ever more rapid growth as some of these communities grew in a helter-skelter way to become thriving cities. Trees were felled, land was leveled, and a checkerboard of streets and avenues evolved. Beauty, light, open space—bare essentials for healthy living—were disregarded in favor of packing people together to keep the wheels of progress turning.

Those who could escape, the well-to-do, fled the city and created second homes for themselves on large tracts in the open countryside. People of more moderate means followed later, slamming their new suburban doors behind them. Only the poor had no option but to remain in the decaying city, in conditions that grew more miserable as housing and services deteriorated.

This, in brief outline, is the story of our older cities, large and small. There is not a long-established urban community in our land that has not experienced this cycle of expansion, desertion, and decay.

Many cities today, however, are showing great powers of rejuvenation. New skyscrapers dot the skyline of every large American city. Some of the older buildings, like the brownstones in New York, are being bought by enterprising people and renovated so that once more they become desirable places to live. But the question still remains as to whether this pattern of birth, unplanned growth, disintegration, and costly rebuilding is the only way to build a city. Might it be possible in coming years to meet the need for more cities by planning them in a life-enhancing, self-renewing way, so that they would grow without disintegrating and age without decaying?

Today no one contemplates building anything on the scale of Chicago or New York. What planners and developers do envision is building many smaller cities of about 50,000 or 100,000 people. These cities would not only provide a good living environment, but would also absorb some of the population and traffic pressure of our older cities. Unlike the suburbs, these cities would house an economically and racially mixed population and they would not depend on the older cities to provide jobs.

These new cities are an experiment. They stem from one man's belief that we can build cities that give people the chance to lead richer, fuller lives. The man's name is Ebenezer Howard and his ideas form the basis of what today is known as the New Town movement.

# Chapter 2 The Launching of the New Town Movement

In 1869, a nineteen-year-old London stenographer named Ebenezer Howard set off with two friends for the western part of the United States. The three hoped to farm and prosper in the vast, open land of America. For such a risky endeavor, however, they appear to have had surprisingly little idea of what they were getting into and where they were going. "At Des Moines, Iowa," wrote Howard, "we were introduced to some Irish-Canadians, and as they had decided to go to Howard County, Nebraska, we went too."

The three Londoners were ill-suited to the rigors of western farming. The enterprise lasted all of three months, after which Howard "turned eastward" for the more hospitable city of Chicago, where he became a stenographer again.

The whole adventure sounds like an expensive waste of time, but it was not. In fact, now, over a hundred years later, we are beginning to accept and follow some of the ideas that were coming to fruition in the mind of that nineteen-year-old youth who was to become the founder of the Garden City movement, which

4

was subsequently renamed the New Town movement.

Ebenezer Howard wrote little about what occurred on his trip and during the next ten years he spent in America. But there is no doubt that his journey had enormous influence on his ideas about town planning. In fact, one of his friends recalls that Howard used to say that he got his ideas for a Garden City while "traveling in America and looking at the wide open spaces." Therefore, it is worthwhile to begin an investigation of the New Town movement in nineteenth century America.

The American West in 1869 was a largely unsettled area. West of Chicago, even along the major routes, vast stretches of land stood empty and untouched by people. "Every ten or fifteen miles," one traveler wrote, "was a stable of the stage proprietor, and every other ten or fifteen miles an eating house; . . . every fifty or one hundred miles we found a small grocery and black-smith shop."

America was land rich. Natural resources abounded. Here, people could start afresh and learn from a history of settlement and city building. Howard was excited by the promise and the opportunity.

He contrasted the large western towns with the London he knew. Chicago, Omaha, and Denver suffered none of the disadvantages of centuries of growth and decay. Each generation in London had to build around the last, and part of the result was visible in large areas of dilapidated housing, squeezed so close together that sunlight was blocked out, and garbage and human wastes blocked in. But in the western United States, a whole city could be planned so that it was not only healthy and hospitable when young, but also able to cope with problems of growth and decay.

What was America doing with this opportunity? Howard saw the answer in the settlements springing up around him. On this open country, settlers simply laid out a grid of streets and built a town. Little thought was given to improving on the cities they had left. These instant towns had a democratic spirit about them and a vitality, but planning went no further than creating an ordered system of streets.

Omaha, Nebraska, near Howard's farm, represented the next stage of city building in the West. In 1865 it was just a settlement, a "feeble rival to Atchison, Leavenworth, and Nebraska City." But with the growth and expansion of the Pacific Railroad, which started in Omaha, it became a great railroad center. Waves of settlers arrived regularly from New England. In 1868, the year before Howard's arrival, Omaha grew spectacularly with the arrival of nearly 15,000 new inhabitants and the construction of 2,500 new buildings. What Ebenezer Howard found was a city of enormous energy, growing so rapidly and chaotically that it was destined to become even more unlivable than London.

More disheartening for Howard, however, must have been the sight of declining towns like the mining town of Austin, Nevada, of which there were many. Austin was described by an American journalist traveling through the West at the time in this way:

> Beginning in 1863, Austin had in a year's time a population of six to eight thousand, fell away in 1865 to four thousand, and now probably has no more than three thousand. Its

houses are built anywhere, everywhere, and then the streets
get to them as best they can; . . . not a tree, not a flower, not
a blade of green grass anywhere in town; . . . but the boot-
black and baths and barbers are of European standards; it
has a first-class French restaurant and a daily paper.

This was how America was taking advantage of its great opportunity. To Ebenezer Howard, even at nineteen, the quality of
the barbers, baths, boot-blacks, and restaurants made little
difference, especially in a place as ugly and unpleasant to live
in as Austin. Whereas the American journalist viewed Austin
simply as a town of the West, Howard saw it as something almost
sinful, which not only could be, but must be improved upon.

Howard learned an important lesson in America and applied
it not only to a scheme for building something more livable than
Austin, but for creating a new kind of city altogether. In his
imagination, kindled by his experience on the frontier, he foresaw
advantages that could be obtained by planning and then building
whole cities at once, from the ground up. The infant towns Howard saw in the United States awakened him to the fact that the
location of cities, their size, and their shape are factors over which
people can have considerable control.

Howard was not alone in his concern about building better
cities, nor was he shy about borrowing other people's ideas. Of
particular importance to him were the precepts of his learned
Scottish contemporary, Patrick Geddes, an ardent spokesman for
environment and man's relation to it. Physical planning, Geddes
felt, had to go hand in hand with social or people planning.

Furthermore, the city ought not to be an isolated entity, but should fit harmoniously into the region of which it is a part. These ideas enriched Howard's thinking and spurred him on.

At nineteen, however, Howard learned mainly from his own observations, which were giving him an awareness of the way cities worked and did not work. He moved to Chicago in 1870 and found its inhabitants struggling to contain and shape their thriving, young city. The flat Midwest provides few natural barriers to check the growth of an expanding city. The Chicago Howard came upon had reached the point at which, if it were to remain a functional unified entity, artificial checks would have to be imposed on its continued expansion.

Enlightened Chicagoans were struggling to do just this, by buying land at the farthest outreaches of the city and setting this property aside as permanent parkland. Howard saw the idea as a good one, especially since it not only would save the city from overexpanding, but would give the city's residents easy access to the beautiful countryside. But how much easier, Howard thought, to impose these boundaries of greenery before a city was built. This meant, of course, knowing or planning in advance how big the city was to be and what shape it should take.

Were people capable of that kind of comprehensive city planning? Were people of the late nineteenth century equipped to do what the Greeks and Romans and American colonials had done, namely to lay out a whole city of limited size in a logical, functional way? Could people also take into account all the complexities of modern civilization, including changes in transportation, communication, and patterns of everyday living? Howard thought they could. The time had come, he felt, to build cities designed to serve their residents, rather than have the residents adjust to the demands and inconveniences of chaotic, endlessly expanding cities.

As an Englishman, Howard was able to contrast what he saw of the new American cities and towns with the old, established cities of England. There was something in the make-up and perceptions of this man that brought him to the combination of ideas—some original, some borrowed—that started the New Town movement. What was he like?

If you had passed Ebenezer Howard on the streets of London, even after he had become Sir Ebenezer Howard, a famous man, he probably would not have caught your eye. He wore wire-rimmed glasses and dressed, as one friend put it, in a "rather shabbily conventional way." In spite of his walrus mustache, he seems to have had a mild, unassuming air about him. In private and business life, one of his colleagues recalls, "his associates tended to disregard him," even when they were working on projects based on his ideas. As George Bernard Shaw, the famous playwright and socialist reformer, remarked, this "amazing man seemed an elderly nobody."

Howard was a Londoner born and bred. He left school and began clerking at the age of fifteen. For most of his life, he earned his living by recording the proceedings of the English court in shorthand. He seems to have been good at his job, fast and meticulous about the way the proceedings were written up.

Before the Garden City idea caught his imagination, Howard spent his evenings and most of his free time working on such inventions as an improvement on the Remington typewriter, a printing press, and a shorthand typewriter. He never made much money on these inventions because the parts cost him more than he received for his finished products. Nevertheless, working through such problems and complications served as a good outlet for his restless mind. His love of inventions also gives a clue to the approach he took toward the Garden City. Like any inventor, he had an overarching idea that he refined and honed piece by piece.

Howard's most noted personal characteristic was his intense preoccupation with his own thoughts. He tended to become so absorbed with a problem or idea that he would forget the day-to-day world. As his wife once remarked, "Of course, he never knows what he is eating so he does not enjoy it; still he never grumbles." In a sense, he was even-tempered by default.

The best illustration of Howard's absent-mindedness is one he supplied himself. "I had gone to Niagara Falls," he wrote, "and as you know, folks can walk to a certain distance underneath them. As I walked, I began going over all sorts of plans for the future, but presently woke to the fact that there was a lot of shouting. I had walked much further than anyone ever was permitted to do and they had been shouting for some time."

Ebenezer Howard was not a good listener. While people were talking to him, he would drift off into a world of his own. At times, however, he could be an effective public speaker. He would become animated with the ideas that obsessed him, and, with a surprisingly rich and powerful voice, could hold an audience. As his biographer wrote, in explaining Howard's ability to enlist

Ebenezer Howard, Garden City pioneer.

support, "He was absolutely convinced that his idea was right. It filled his mind. . . . He impressed people as a transparently honest man who ought to be helped make good."

With his absent-mindedness and detachment from the humdrum world, Howard was not a good administrator. But these same traits served him well in framing his plans for the Garden City. He cared for the big problems and did not get bogged down in details. He did not, for example, try to figure out where each tree should be planted or how wide each street should be. In part, his Garden City ideas are still useful because they are flexible. His suggestions are confined to the bare outlines and to the essential aspects of town design, leaving room for changes in accordance with new ideas.

An unusual person founded the New Town movement. Ebenezer Howard had little formal schooling and no training in anything relating to architecture or town planning. In fact, there is nothing in his background that explains why he should have become interested in building cities. But he did.

Basically, Howard had stumbled on the field of city planning and found himself at home there. Once he began to explore the ways cities usually sprang up—in topsy-turvy fashion—and the ways they might be created, with forethought, he lost interest in almost everything else. City planning captivated his mind; the underlying ideas fascinated him. Soon he began to synthesize these ideas and to give them an original form. Finally, he came up with a new approach to building cities, an approach that was not only different from anything that had come before, but that marked the beginning of an entirely new movement in city planning.

Certainly, Howard's adventures in America sparked his imagination and gave him many insights. His desire to improve the conditions of workers in London gave him added incentive to perfect his ideas and to try to put them into practice. But, essentially, these are factors that influenced his thinking; they do not explain the final synthesis. This came from the inner vision of a man who could look at the problems of the city and of rural life with new eyes and fresh ideas—someone who could see beyond the individual structures to the city as a whole. Howard had this kind of perceptiveness. He was able to visualize not only a better city, but a new kind of city—a "New Town."

Lewis Mumford, the famous sociologist, urbanist, and writer, speaks of Howard as "the English mind at its best: always in touch with the practicable, always in sight of the ideal." It was an inventor's mind. He started with a problem, worked it over until he thought he had a solution, then drew up a blueprint, and finally built a working model to test his idea. By 1898, his Garden City idea had reached the blueprint stage. He published this proposed solution to the problem of people living in crowded, unhealthy cities in a book called *Tomorrow: A Peaceful Path to Real Reform*, which was reissued in 1902 as *Garden Cities of Tomorrow*. The book is more than a collection of good ideas; it contains the plans for a Garden City.

"At the beginning of the twentieth century two great inventions took form before our eyes: the aeroplane and the Garden City, both harbingers of a new age." So writes Lewis Mumford in what seems an unusual if not an incongruous comparison. If we do not fly every day, our letters do, while many of us have never heard of a Garden City, much less felt that it was an important force giving shape to our age.

Mumford's comparison, however, has merit, because it highlights the nature and scope of the Garden City, the forerunner of the New Town. Like the airplane, the Garden City is an invention. Thus, while the technological problems of building a plane are very different from the human problems of building a city, the approaches used in both instances are similar. The Wright brothers came up with an idea, built a plane, and flew it. Similarly, Ebenezer Howard refined his ideas, built Letchworth Garden City as his first working model, and in that way demonstrated the viability of his ideas.

The potential impact of the Garden City may also have the kind of epoch-shaping dimensions of the airplane. We think of the world differently now that air flight makes distant cities so few hours away. Similarly, our civilization would change considerably with the growth of small, self-sufficient cities instead of suburbs. This has already begun to happen in England, where it is estimated that one in every twenty persons will be living in a New Town in 1981. The increased livability of London, which has stopped expanding ever outward by adding suburb after suburb, is one important result.

Ebenezer Howard developed the Garden City idea as a solution to the problem of overcrowded cities, with their inherent drawbacks. In the 1890s, as is the case today, people were leaving the small towns and countryside to find work in the large cities. Howard saw this migration and the resulting congestion as something deplorable. To reverse this trend, or at least to change its character, he proposed that we counter the pull of the city with something that is even more attractive.

What, he asked, makes a city alluring—why is it a magnet that draws such large numbers of people? He set down a list of reasons: "Social opportunities, high money wages, chance of employment, well-lit streets." But the city also has drawbacks. These included: "Closing out of nature, isolation of crowds, high rents and high prices, fogs and droughts, costly drainage and slums." Howard then analyzed the advantages and disadvantages of country living and discovered that it had exactly the opposite attractions and drawbacks. In the country, a person can suffer from "a lack of society, low wages, few social opportunities, and difficulty getting work." The country dweller, however, has in abundance most things the city person lacks: "The beauty of nature, fresh air, low rents, bright sunshine, and clean water." If people, Howard concluded, could combine the advantages of the city and the country and eliminate most of the drawbacks, they would have something far more desirable than either.

Howard proposed to do this in what he called a Garden City. If he could build a large number of Garden Cities, he thought, people would leave the overcrowded cities and move to the new ones. Furthermore, people would move by choice.

In his book, *Garden Cities of Tomorrow,* Howard explains how it is economically possible to build this "town-country magnet," this Garden City. Howard's economic argument is particularly important because his primary aim was to build good housing that workers could afford. The system of speculative building on individual sites, he felt, produces intolerable housing and living conditions for people with small incomes. Thus, a new and more economical system of building was essential in order to create better living conditions for people in general and for working-class people in particular.

The essence of Howard's plan is to control the enormous increase in the price of land when a rural area becomes urbanized. First, one must buy a large block of land, say 6,000 acres. By purchasing farmland or undeveloped land in a rural area one should be able to buy it at low cost. The purchaser can be an individual or a corporation, but in either case would be limited to a profit of five percent annually. This keeps the price of lots from doubling again and again as the Garden City develops, as is the case in most growing towns. The housing, the cost of shop rentals, and everything else in the Garden City should therefore be cheaper than in a conventional town, because the basic cost of land would be much less expensive.

The second part of Howard's economic argument is that building a Garden City on vacant land is economical because construction costs can be radically reduced. Valuable time can be saved getting equipment to and from the site since there would be no narrow congested roads or crowded open-air markets to block the way. The biggest and most efficient equipment can be used because the massive scale of building could keep the machines working to capacity. Neighbors would not complain about the machinery being noisy or disruptive because there would be no neighbors. There would also be no old buildings to tear down before erecting new ones.

Costs for materials and production procedures are cheaper when a contractor builds ten houses instead of one, and cheaper still when he builds a hundred. In the building of a Garden City, no roads have to be torn up to put down pipes. By knowing in advance the proper size and placement for utilities like sewer pipes and electric cables, the residents of the Garden City should benefit from better services at lower costs than the people in most towns, where these conveniences are added as their city grows.

Howard's argument for rational planning in advance and for single ownership of the land is a good one, but the scheme requires a tremendous initial investment with no return on the money until people, shops, and industry move into the town. Raising the initial capital is further complicated by the problem of attracting the residents. It is impossible to get people to settle in a town until there are shops and jobs, and it is impossible to attract shops and industry until there are people.

Howard's book also deals with the shape and functioning of the Garden City. He begins with four theoretical ideas about how to build a better city. The first is that all the land should be under single ownership and that the city should be planned in advance. Interestingly, he anticipated modern town planning practices by insisting that the planning not be done by a single individual. The town plan, he believed, should be the product of a "teamwork of many minds: architects, engineers, medical men, sanitation experts, landscape gardeners, etc."

His second general idea arose from his conception of the city as something organic, "like a flower or a tree or an animal." Not only must a town grow in a balanced way and be self-sustaining at every stage, but it must finally reach a desired size and then stop growing. Howard figured a good size for a Garden City as about 1,000 acres. A city of that size is small enough so that the residents can walk to work, to shops, or to school. It is large enough to accommodate 32,000 people in houses and cottages, with space for private gardens.

Howard's third proposal was that a "greenbelt" of farms and open countryside should surround the residential and industrial areas where most of the people live. As much as 5,000 acres of land might go into making up this greenbelt, which could include an agricultural college, pastures for sheep and cows, and a forest for wildlife, in addition to parks. The greenbelt provides the people living in the central, urban portion of the Garden City with country experiences, such as the seasonal ones of seedtime and harvest. The greenbelt is also a place for solitude and refuge. In addition, the nearness of town and country benefits farmers and others working in the greenbelt. They have a nearby market for their produce and a place to go to counter the isolation of rural living. Last, the greenbelt serves as a buffer around the town. It checks the growth of suburbs, insuring that the Garden City not grow beyond a predetermined size.

Finally, the Garden City Howard envisioned is to be a balanced community including industrial, commercial, residential and cultural facilities. The industry and shops provide jobs for the people living in the town. In this way the town is self-contained and self-sufficient. It is also linked to the outside world by a railroad (the Model T Ford was still ten years away), conveniently located, to provide the town residents with transportation and the town industries with goods and supplies.

Howard was an inventor and planner at least as much as he was a visionary and a utopian. In addition to his theoretical ideas about a Garden City, he was very specific about what a Garden City might look like. He worked out a number of diagrams which are the first, if not the final, sketches for a real city. They are not as detailed as architectural prints or a master plan, and they are too general for any specific site. (Howard always added the cautionary label to each diagram: "Plan must depend on the site selected.") But they are concrete enough and close enough to the actual plans for a city to crystallize Howard's theories and make them coherent and applicable.

In order to minimize the distance between all points and make it a city for walkers, Howard sketched out a circular Garden City. At the very center he put a garden surrounded by the important public buildings, such as the town hall, the library, and the hospital. Six roads were to radiate from the center, dividing the town into wards that were meant to develop into neighborhoods. The Garden City was further defined by a series of circular roads surrounding the center in concentric rings. The commercial and shopping area would be clustered around the circular road nearest the town center. The last circular road, on the outskirts of the town, would be part of the industrial zone containing factories, warehouses, and coal yards. Both the people of the town and the industry would benefit from this kind of planning, Howard maintained: industry because it was near the railroad lines; the residential part of the community because it

# EBENEZER HOWARD'S PLAN FOR A GARDEN CITY

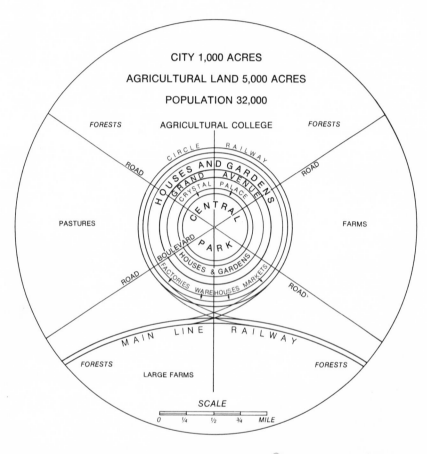

CITY 1,000 ACRES

AGRICULTURAL LAND 5,000 ACRES

POPULATION 32,000

FORESTS          AGRICULTURAL COLLEGE          FORESTS

CIRCLE     RAILWAY

ROAD                                        ROAD

HOUSES AND GARDENS

GRAND AVENUE

CRYSTAL PALACE

PASTURES          CENTRAL          FARMS

PARK

BOULEVARD

HOUSES & GARDENS

ROAD     FACTORIES WAREHOUSES MARKETS     ROAD

MAIN     LINE     RAILWAY

FORESTS          FORESTS

LARGE FARMS

SCALE

0     ¼     ½     ¾     MILE

— Six roads radiate from cenve.
divides city into wards.

How Letchworth Differed: 
- not as many greenbelts
- railroad through middle
- not exact shapes (ie 6)
- No park in centre

← No park

## ONE SECTION OF HOWARD'S PROPOSED GARDEN CITY

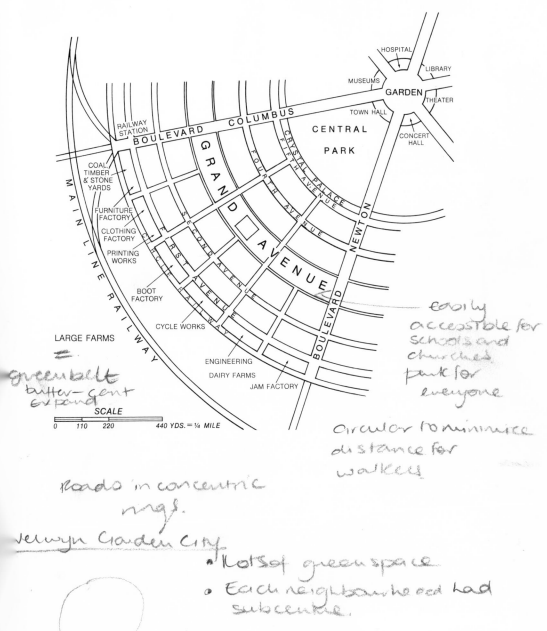

HOSPITAL
LIBRARY
MUSEUMS
GARDEN
THEATER
TOWN HALL
CENTRAL
PARK
CONCERT
HALL
RAILWAY STATION
BOULEVARD COLUMBUS
GRAND
CRYSTAL PALACE
FOURTH AVENUE
FIFTH AVENUE
NEWTON
COAL, TIMBER & STONE YARDS
FURNITURE FACTORY
CLOTHING FACTORY
PRINTING WORKS
SECOND AVENUE
AVENUE
BOULEVARD
MAIN LINE RAILWAY
FIRST AVENUE
CIRCLE RAILWAY
BOOT FACTORY
CYCLE WORKS
ENGINEERING
DAIRY FARMS
JAM FACTORY
LARGE FARMS

SCALE
0   110   220      440 YDS. = ¼ MILE

greenbelt
butter—cent
expand

easily accessible for schools and churches
park for everyone

circular to minimize distance for walkers

Roads in concentric rings.

Welwyn Garden City
- Lots of green space
- Each neighbourhood had subcentre.

was insulated from the smoke, noise, and traffic connected with industry.

One important innovation for which Howard alone seems responsible is the concentric strip of open land running half-way between the town center and the industrial zone. This "Grand Avenue" can serve as a convenient park for all the residents as well as an ideal location for the schools and churches. Running through the middle of the residential part of the city, it is easily accessible to all the houses.

Howard did not confine himself to the physical plan of the Garden City. His mind swept over the whole spectrum of community life, and he often found startlingly simple ways to improve on existing patterns. In the commercial zone, for example, he hoped to set up a "Crystal Palace," a large glass-enclosed building to serve as a shopping center. He also wanted it to be a place people would enjoy visiting. The problem was how to have all kinds of shops and still have enough space for features like fountains, a roller-skating rink, and a summer and winter garden with benches and places to stroll.

Howard's solution was to save space by initially allowing only one shop of any kind. However, a storeowner's position as the only person who sold shoes or hardware would last only as long as he maintained the goodwill of his customers. Howard imagined telling a potential shopkeeper, "If the people become dissatisfied with your methods of trading, then, on requisition of a certain number, the necessary space in the Arcade will be allotted . . . to someone desirous of starting an opposition store."

The remarkable thing about *Garden Cities of Tomorrow* is

Howard's precise focus on what he himself could contribute and what things were better left to others. He knew he was not an architect or even a city planner in the strict sense of being able to fit buildings to the topography and drainage patterns of the land. He therefore kept his designs general and left the specifics to others who, he readily acknowledged, were better equipped to translate his ideas into a real city. He balanced the role of theorist and that of planner in such a way that his ideas were specific, but their application flexible.

In the last chapter of *Garden Cities of Tomorrow*, Howard lays out his grand scheme for the creation of "Social Cities." The Garden City is the basic unit of design, but it is integrated into a larger entity. Howard understood the advantages of large cities, particularly as cultural, economic, and governmental centers. But, he felt, they should not grow as a solid mass in which people at the center are closed in and cut off from the countryside. His Social City, therefore, depends on an unusually large Garden City, the "Central City." Like any other Garden City, the Central City is surrounded by a greenbelt, but at the outskirts of this open land, Howard envisioned a circle of other Garden Cities. These outer cities would be connected to the Central City and to each other by a high speed railroad, but separated by their contiguous greenbelts. This leapfrog expansion of the Social City would create a system similar to a planet—the Central City with its orbiting moons.

Howard's Social City has yet to be built. In England today, established cities like London and Manchester act as Central Cities, and are encircled at a distance with New Towns.

Letchworth, England, was the first working model of a Garden City, inspired by Howard's book and by Howard himself. Though it is not the realization of his grand scheme, as people often tend to think, it is a remarkable step in the translation of many of his ideas into a Garden City where real people live and work.

# Chapter 3  The Original New Towns

The Letchworth story begins in 1898 with the publication of *Garden Cities of Tomorrow*. The book came at a favorable time. English reform groups were enjoying great popularity and many people were ready to give serious consideration to an innovative idea like Howard's.

Land-nationalization groups, for example, had gained significant followings, by pointing out the evils of land speculation. These groups were angered by the huge profits that speculators made by buying land and then simply holding it and allowing it to increase in value. Land, they argued, was a national resource and should be used for the benefit of all citizens, not as an investment by which the rich get richer. Howard's scheme appealed to these people because, as we have seen, it attempted to keep the price of land in the Garden City from increasing or, at least, to use the increase for the benefit of the residents and not for investment gains.

Howard's book also appealed to the Quakers and to reform groups concerned about the condition of the working class. The

Fabian Society in London was a socialist group of middle- and upper-class intellectuals who urged the government to take a more active role in improving the treatment and living conditions of workers. For them, Howard's book offered a practical way of improving working-class housing and alleviating urban congestion. Howard's plan was not the full scale reform they were looking for, just as it was not a full scale land-nationalization program, but the Fabians endorsed the idea by and large, and some members bought stock in the first Garden City venture.

When Howard's book was published, it circulated through various reform groups, attracting considerable interest and a small number of adherents. These adherents grouped together and, eight months after publication, formed a Garden City Association. The purpose of the Association was to spread Howard's ideas and to begin laying the groundwork for the actual construction of a Garden City.

A year after the publication of Howard's book, Garden Cities were still nothing but an idea. Yet something extraordinary seemed to be happening. Instead of dismissing Howard's fantastic idea of a Garden City as an unobtainable goal, people were attracted by its heroic proportions and by the sheer force of a good idea. Instead of asking where the money would come from, they were saying, "The Garden City sounds like a good idea. Let's build one!" And Ebenezer Howard was not standing idly by. He did not have the money to begin to build a city, but he had his vision, and he was promoting it to anyone who would listen.

After the Garden City Association was formed, one of the first and most important people to come into the fold was Ralph Neville. This prominent lawyer, later a judge, read Howard's book and found the ideas so sensible that he wrote an article about Garden Cities. Howard sought him out and persuaded him to join the Garden City Association. With his distinguished reputation, Neville greatly enhanced the credibility of the organization. He also proved to be an invaluable leader when it came to practical matters like administration and fund raising.

In 1900 the members of the Garden City Association felt ready to embark on their great undertaking—the building of a Garden City. The Association created a non-profit corporation to find a site. This pioneer company, First Garden City, Ltd., acted swiftly and dramatically. It selected and investigated a large number of sites and chose the most suitable one.

The actual purchase of the site required some daring and intrigue, because the desired piece of land was made up of several farms controlled by fifteen different owners. If any one of them had found out what was going on, he would have held out and forced the corporation to pay an unreasonably high price. But, purchase by purchase, the corporation unobtrusively acquired these moderate-size farms until it had assembled a unified piece of property encompassing 3,918 acres (later increased to 4,574 acres). In just three years the coporation had taken the Garden City idea over its first big hurdle. The company now owned land only thirty-four miles from London, with sufficient water resources for a future city and with a close link to Great Britain's major north-south railroad line.

The next step was to plan a Garden City. Howard's concepts would serve as guiding principles, but someone with experience in architecture and planning was needed to take these ideas and apply them to the Letchworth estate. In 1903, Howard and the other members of the Board of Directors of First Garden City, Ltd. opened a competition to choose a planner. From the sketchy plans for a future Letchworth submitted by a number of architects, they selected Raymond Unwin and Barry Parker.

Their Letchworth plan was based on the fact that the city would be of limited size. It would not be circular in shape, as Howard had suggested, because the Letchworth estate was not round; but Unwin and Parker still tried to follow the intent behind Howard's circular plan—to create a city for walkers. The planners did this by locating the essential services of the city in a central place, within walking distance of all the housing.

The first real decision that Unwin and Parker had to make was how many acres to devote to the urban part of the Garden City and how much to the greenbelt. Howard had suggested roughly 1,000 acres for the city and 5,000 for the greenbelt. Unwin and Parker began with this estimate, but calculated that because the size of British families was getting smaller and also because Howard had made an error in his estimating procedures, 1,000 acres would provide housing for only 16,000 people. A 16,000-person city, they knew, would be too small to generate enough money in rent to pay for the whole Letchworth estate. There would also be too few people, the planners felt, to complete the kind of city that Howard envisioned. So they redrew their design, devoting about 3,000 acres to urban necessities and leaving the remainder as greenbelt. This meant that the greenbelt would never be as dominant as Howard had envisioned, but would still serve such purposes as limiting the size of the city and giving it a buffer of greenery for the residents to enjoy.

Next came the question of industry. Industrial enterprises must be built on flat land. It is also important, in planning for industry, to calculate which way the wind usually blows so that smoke-producing factories do not fill the residential and commercial parts of the city with fumes.

There was another important consideration about the placement of industry: what to do with the railroad tracks that bisected the Letchworth estate and that would serve as the major supply and shipping source for the factories. Unwin and Parker could either work with these existing tracks and incorporate them into their plan, or they could seek permission to rip them up and build a new set at the outskirts of town. They decided that the expense and difficulty of rebuilding the railroad overruled that option. The planners left the tracks as they were and created industrial parks in the flat land alongside them, rather than at the periphery of the town. This compromise did not really go against Howard's overall aims, they felt, because their plan still kept industry from being noisy and obtrusive, and from disrupting the residential traffic. Unwin and Parker believed they had maintained the functional aspects of Howard's plans while changing some of its superficial features.

Finally, the planners had to decide where to place residential zones, parks, and the town center. Geological factors played an important role in these decisions. Unwin and Parker had to consider the natural drainage patterns of the land. They had to avoid interfering with the water supply for the city, and they had to evaluate the different kinds of soil on the estate. This information was needed to determine the best areas for building and the parts of the estate that would be swampy or otherwise inadequate for building. Howard's circular city, with its radiating streets, did not allow as much flexibility as Unwin and Parker wanted for fitting the buildings to the contours of the land and its geological features. Besides, with the changes they had made in the size of the city and the new placement of the industrial zones, other adjustments in Howard's plan would be necessary. So the planners again substituted their own design, aiming to achieve the goals that had stimulated Howard to draw up a circular city. Instead of pie-shaped wards, Parker and Unwin decided to divide the city into amorphous-shaped, residential groupings that they hoped would develop into neighborhoods. Each neighborhood would be set off from the others by open land—a place for recreation and play. Each neighborhood would also be situated so that it was within walking distance of the town center.

In 1904 these plans were substantially completed and the founders of Letchworth had a map showing them where roads, houses, and industry should go. But how was the corporation going to raise the money to build them? The rapid progress in choosing and buying a site before sufficient funds were in hand to complete the project had been Howard's doing. He was anxious to get the Garden City going, and he pushed and prodded his colleagues to be daring.

The Garden City Corporation, however, was at a disadvantage in trying to raise sufficient money on the open market. Howard's proposition was a laudable ideal—that the increased value of the land and the savings from large scale, planned development should be used for the benefit of future residents and not for the benefit of investors. But what it meant in practical terms was that the Garden City Corporation was offering the public the chance to put money into a risky venture in which the investor could make only a five percent profit.

No one interested in obtaining a large, or even a safe, return on his investment—the usual reasons for investing—would want to sink money into this project. Those who bought stock in First Garden City, Ltd. did so because they were committed to the new idea. The people who had a real stake in Letchworth— the workers for whom it was being built—could not afford to invest in the venture. Money had to come from wealthy reformers who believed in Howard's idea or from friends of Ralph Neville's who could be coaxed into buying a few shares. Some of the people who bought stock became so interested in the Garden City idea that they later bought a house and joined the experiment, but most bought stock because they thought a Garden City should be built. These were people willing to risk a little money on the venture.

It is to the great credit of the founders of Letchworth that they raised as much money as they did. A year after the acquisition of the land for Letchworth Garden City, First Garden City, Ltd. had raised almost a half-million dollars (£100,000). But, impressive as this was, it did not even pay the purchase price on the land.

The next step, therefore, was to mortgage the land, to give the founders money to complete the purchase and to do the beginning work on drainage, water works, and land development. But where was the money to come from to build an entire Garden

City? Who would pay the enormous costs of bringing in the most efficient machinery, of building large numbers of houses quickly and cheaply, as Howard had proposed? The answer was no one.

A year after the purchase of the estate, the only money that was coming into the corporation was rent from the farmers who continued to farm there, and trickles of cash from the continued sale of stock. But this sum was barely adequate to meet the taxes and mortgage payments on the land. One local builder leased some of the land and put up six cottages, but he had trouble selling them and this discouraged the onlooking builders who might have been willing to construct houses on land they did not own. The Garden City experiment thus threatened to collapse into bankruptcy. The questions being discussed by the leaders of the Garden City movement were no longer about what Letchworth should look like or how it should be built, but which of the Garden City principles to abandon.

At this crucial juncture, Thomas Adams, the first manager of Letchworth, got in touch with J. St. Loe Strachey, an influential newspaper and magazine editor and a supporter of the Garden City idea. Together, they arranged to have an already proposed exhibition called "Cheap Cottages for Agricultural Workers" held at Letchworth. One hundred and twenty-one cottages were built for the exhibition and these remained on the site and became the biggest part of the early town. Thousands of visitors came to see the exhibition, which demonstrated that good housing could be built inexpensively. The curious also came to see what a Garden City looked like.

The cottage that won first prize is still in use, along with a number of others. It was built for £150, approximately $730. Workers could afford to rent or buy these houses, and they began to move in. So did three factories, including the Garden City Press. By 1906, 173 acres in Letchworth were occupied. In 1907, there were approximately 400 families in residence. The first Garden City was finally under way.

The story of Letchworth's growth from then till now is one of gradual development. The continual shortage of money and the massive debts meant that houses were never put up in large numbers. However, as the town grew and more industry came, it became easier to sell houses and, therefore, easier to find people willing to build them. The corporation also had the task of constructing roads and installing utility lines, which never came as fast as they were needed. All in all, the process of building Letchworth was not the one Howard had envisioned, but it did follow the guidelines of the Parker and Unwin plan and certainly deserves to be called the first Garden City.

Before evaluating Letchworth's successes and failures and describing what it looks like today, one should try to capture some of the spirit of the place in its early days. The life blood of a city is not buildings and land plans; it is people. And how can one tell the story of Letchworth without talking about what it was like to live there? Mr. Arthur Lamb, who is now in semi-retirement, still has a vivid memory of the early days in Letchworth.

"In 1907, when we first moved to Letchworth," Mr. Lamb recalled, "there were only four hundred people. The estate was still mostly farmland, so we had to find lodging in the nearby village of Baldock and wait for a house to be built."

In the early days, he remembers, "School was conducted in the temporary huts which had been used to house the workers building the first roads in Letchworth." Mr. Lamb continued, "Letchworth attracted a great variety of people, from the artists and craftsmen to the architects who came and built their own homes. Above all," he concluded, "it attracted idealists."

The people who lasted had to deal with many practical problems they had not forseen, because Letchworth in those days lacked the resources to cope fully with matters like water supply, sewage, gas, and electricity. The first inhabitants also learned to live with such inconveniences as muddy roads, inadequate internal transportation, and poor shopping facilities, for stores came even more slowly than people. "But we had an interesting time of it and a big social life," Mr. Lamb went on. "People would trek across fields and along muddy roads by lantern light to the meeting house, where they would arrange all kinds of interesting activities."

Today, Letchworth is an established town of 32,000 people. Newcomers find that it has lost some of its uniqueness, because it is no longer struggling for survival or engaged in a bold, new experiment.

Letchworth, like every other city, tells its own story in its buildings, its use of land, and its people. Letchworth's struggle for survival is recorded in its lack of frills. The houses are made of a local brick covered with cement plaster, the building materials most prevalent in that part of the country. These substances are strong and durable, but have a rather drab appearance. They bear witness to the urgent need for economy in building and the attempt to get the most out of the available resources.

The distinguishing feature that gives a kind of unity to the town is the sharp slant of the roofs on all the buildings, remnants of the Edwardian period when Letchworth was started. And Letchworth's encircling greenery is still there, ensuring that the city does not expand beyond its preplanned size.

One of the great advantages of being able to plan a whole city in advance is that the planners are able to decide exactly how many and what kind of houses should be built to balance the need for privacy with the need to save money and land. The planners can also design the rest of the city so that parks are near the residences, not only providing play space but giving the whole area a feeling of openness. In Letchworth, Unwin and Parker were extremely sensitive to these considerations. Thus, in spite of its high-density housing, as compared with most modern suburbs, Letchworth does not seem cramped and no one complains of feeling closed in by neighbors.

There are ninety-four factories in Letchworth, located mainly near the railroad tracks, and almost every resident is able to find a job within the town itself. In fact, Letchworth, more than any other Garden City or New Town, has maintained Howard's ideal of providing work for its residents during all stages of the town's growth.

The most obvious shortcomings of Letchworth can be seen in the town center. There was no money for a grand arcade, as Howard envisioned, so shops settled in one at a time, making an overall plan impossible. The idea of a village green at the center was unfortunately never tried. Instead, there is a railroad station. In this downtown area and elsewhere, the planners did institute some architectural controls to ensure that no buildings were particularly ugly or outlandish, but even this effort met with bitter opposition from individual builders, who were not used to having any checks on their designs.

All in all, Unwin and Parker seem to have done well at predicting and anticipating the future needs and future growth of Letchworth. It is a tribute to the original design and to the concept of planning a city in advance that the plan for Letchworth, set down in 1903 and 1904, has stood up as well as it has. The three major criticisms of Letchworth voiced by its citizens have been: poor shopping facilities, too much industry, and inadequate space for cars. The latter flaw is particularly evident in the town center, where the streets are narrow and getting through them or finding a place to park is quite difficult. Letchworth was planned and built just before the advent of the car.

Unlike many cities its size and age, Letchworth can look forward to a future brighter than its past. Howard's hypothesis that normal and even low rents would eventually pay off the debt, and leave the town with surplus money, has proven true. In 1972, the Letchworth Development Corporation, which replaced First Garden City, Ltd., found itself with a surplus of $78,000. As a nonprofit corporation, and in accordance with Howard's principles, the company is required to turn this money back into the town. Moreover, this accumulation of excess money is not a one-time occurrence; it should happen yearly as the Letchworth debt decreases. As one member of the development corporation stated, "Letchworth has never been and will never be a museum piece."

Letchworth has not been without its critics, particularly people living in the long-established, nearby village of Hitchin. One resident, Ronald Hine, even went so far as to put his opinion into verse:

> God the first garden made,
> And the first city Cain,
> Deep in a proverb thus 'twas laid,
> Profound, precise and plain.
> But garden-cities, garden-cities!
> Who the deuce makes garden-cities?
> Will someone please explain? . . .
> For then we'd know, for weal or woe,
> Where all these mad mixed-blessings flow,
> And folk would be no more perplext,
> With that dark thought they are now vext,
> Is God or Man to blame?

The day after he published this piece, Mr. Hine received the following postcard from Ebenezer Howard. "You need not blame God, if anyone, it is I who am to blame. I promise to do better next time." Fifteen years later, Howard began to fulfill his promise.

In 1918 he took two of his closest associates, Frederic Osborn and C. B. Purdom, for a walk over the present site of Welwyn Garden City. The trip, as Osborn recalls, "was to convince us that the site was suitable . . . in case we were challenged when lecturing (as we often were) to show that possible sites existed." This very land came on the market in May, 1919, entirely by chance, but, as Osborn writes: "Howard, I think, saw in this coincidence the finger of destiny."

A few days before the sale of the land, Howard could count on pledges of about $4,800 "that had been promised if I made a second effort to build a Garden City." So, his biographer quotes him as saying, "I got busy on the telephone and by ten o'clock had another 2,000 pounds [about $9,600] promised. . . . That was 10 percent of the purchase price, enough to pay the deposit. So I went to the sale, made my bid and secured the second Garden City."

Howard, then seventy years old, felt that if he wanted his Garden Cities built, he would have to build them. "If we wait for the State," he wrote, "nothing will be done." The government did, however, come into the picture soon after the purchase of land for Welwyn. In 1921, the Garden City movement was given recognition in a report to Parliament about improving the living conditions of British workers. As part of the Housing Act of 1921, the Public Loan Board was empowered to make loans to "authorized associations" involved in building Garden Cities. The existence of Letchworth helped convince a Parliamentary commission that a Garden City could be a sensible investment. Welwyn became the first authorized association and secured loans of various sizes during its early development.

This financing enabled Welwyn Garden City, Ltd. to assume a much larger role in shaping the city than was the case at Letchworth. Where First Garden City, Ltd. confined itself to land development and the main public services, the Welwyn corporation and its subsidiaries became involved in electricity, transportation, theater, gravel and brick works, and day nurseries. The most controversial project undertaken by the Corporation, however, was the Welwyn store.

Rather than repeat the experience at Letchworth, where the first stores had to be given long-term leases at very low rents, the founders of Welwyn decided not to rent any commercial space at all. Instead, they set up a huge department store to supply everything from shirts to lawnmowers. The store was given a monopoly (to extend no more than ten years), so that it could do a volume of business large enough to make up for all the seldom-used items it was required to stock. People complained during those early years of a lack of choice, but by using this system, Welwyn was not forced to squander its valuable commercial property. When Welwyn eventually opened the door to other stores, the town was in a commanding position and could be more selective about where stores should go and how they should look. More than that, the corporation was able to charge reasonable rents on short-term leases, rents that could be increased as the city grew and prospered.

The planning of Welwyn was substantially different from the planning of Letchworth. Instead of two architect-planners like Unwin and Parker, who constructed an overall plan, Welwyn was designed by a team of specialists, each of whom knew a particular aspect of city planning and could assess the problems and possibilities in every proposed scheme.

The Welwyn planners used the Letchworth design as a starting point and tried to improve on it. They came up with a plan that had many of the same features as Letchworth: a greenbelt, an industrial zone near the railroad tracks, and a maximum of twelve dwellings to the residential acre. The Welwyn plan differed from Letchworth, however, in that it set aside more land as permanent open space. The Welwyn plan also included a shield of trees forty to fifty feet wide between the industrial and residential zones. In addition, the planners extended the concept of the neighborhood unit by creating subcenters with shops, schools, and churches as an integral part of each neighborhood.

Welwyn most noticeably improved on Letchworth in the design of the town center. The Welwyn planners were able to get much closer to Howard's original concept of a park at the center of town. In the downtown area of Welwyn they placed a tree-lined walking area with benches. Near the Howard Memorial and the central fountain, a magnificent vista opens in both directions. Even in the town center, the planners succeeded in merging the advantages of the city and the delights of the country, as Howard had hoped.

Welwyn today, with its natural beauty and its feeling of openness, comes close to Howard's idea of a city within a garden. The planners took advantage of natural resources such as the abundance of material to make red Hertfordshire brick. These bricks make for elegantly defined buildings and houses. Welwyn's careful planning also accents the natural beauty of the rolling countryside in which the town is located.

In recent years, Welwyn's charm has been further enhanced

Welwyn's planned town center.

by the addition of recreational facilities that were not in the original Welwyn plan. They show the flexibility possible even in a city that is planned in advance. The most spectacular additions, at the outskirts of town, are two artificial lakes which have been dredged out for boating and sailing. An even more creative project has been the conversion of the old pit where material for brick-making was once dug, into something more than a scar on the land. The pit has been enlarged and is now the foundation of an athletic stadium that fits attractively into the earth. And, one of the banks of this same pit is used as the base for an artificial ski slope.

Welwyn Garden City is not a country club suburb. It is a flourishing Garden City. People with a wide variety of incomes live there. Welwyn's hundred factories provide jobs for almost all of its inhabitants. And, though it has remained close to the size of Howard's model, with over 42,000 people in 1973, and a final projection of 50,000, Welwyn appears to have sufficient activities and liveliness for the people who live there, and even for a stream of newcomers from London. "People move here from London in order to get work, but they take the twenty mile train ride back each weekend for about the first month," one of the members of the town's commission told us. "Then their trips begin to get less and less regular, and, after about three to six months, they are having their London friends and relatives up here."

Sir Frederic Osborn, who is in many ways Ebenezer Howard's successor as the leading exponent of the Garden City idea, has lived in Welwyn since it began, and still lives there in a modest-size, older house. He has written extensively on New Towns, and was instrumental in making their creation a national policy in Great Britain.

Sir Frederic Osborn feels that Welwyn turned out as its founders had hoped. Though it lacks some of the technological innovations of cities that have been designed since, Welwyn is a good example of a city suited to the needs and desires of the people who live there. In fact, Osborn declared with a smile, "We learned from and improved on Letchworth, but no New Town in England has improved on us!"

Other residents hold similar views. "For some of my neighbors," one of them remarked, "their loyalty and love of Welwyn approaches patriotism."

Nine years after the founding of Welwyn, Ebenezer Howard died, and no one else was willing to take the initiative and risks of starting another New Town. In 1937, however, Prime Minister Neville Chamberlain became concerned about the way London was continuing to grow and swell. He appointed a Royal Commission to study the situation. Two years later, the commission delivered a report advocating the building of a group of government sponsored New Towns around London to absorb some of its excess population.

World War II interrupted further developments, but in 1944 another report, entitled the "Greater London Plan," came out. It suggested that London could be made more manageable and human by accentuating the existing neighborhoods and giving them physical definition. By using a system of parks and other perimeter barriers, the report went on to say, it would be possible to convert London into a group of distinct, though closely interconnected, communities of defined size and character. The report also proposed dispersing one million people from London, and a lesser number from most of the other large cities, into a group of New Towns and "country town extensions."

These two reports provided the impetus for the New Towns Act passed in 1946. This historic bill made New Towns a national policy. It gave the government the power to set up government-financed, public corporations. Each corporation would be responsible for building a single New Town and would be given the authority to buy the land it needed, by direct purchase or by condemning and then buying it at a reasonable price.

The prime goal of the New Town program has been to get people out of the worst parts of the large cities to the New Towns. The British Trade Board has jurisdiction over the choice of sites for industrial expansion, a power which is utilized to draw factories to the New Towns. People follow the jobs, with preference for housing given to those living in the overcrowded central cities. In fact, with a continued housing shortage, the British Government is able to stipulate that you have to have a job in a New Town before you can get a house there, though, once you are there, losing or quitting a job does not mean losing your house.

One of the early problems in the New Towns was a pervasive feeling of uprootedness, which the British press labeled "the New Town blues." Moving from familiar neighborhoods into a town where everyone was a stranger could not help but be a disorienting experience. The New Town planners, however, came up with two imaginative responses that have at least lessened this problem. One was to try to supply housing to the parents or children of anyone living in a New Town. The second idea was to build New Towns around existing small towns. Although this latter practice cuts down on the flexibility of the New Town design, it does give people the comfortable feeling of being part of an old, established community.

Since 1946, twenty-eight New Towns have been started. Today, they house over three quarters of a million people. And each has remained faithful to Howard's central principles.

The development of New Towns and other dispersal procedures has enabled the government to put a greenbelt around London to keep it from expanding outward. London has not become any smaller, so the program is not a complete success. Furthermore, the New Towns of England and Scotland have absorbed only about ten percent of the population growth that has taken place in these countries since World War II. Even newer and more comprehensive planning is necessary, and the British government has now embarked on a region-by-region planning program that analyzes the anticipated growth in each section of the country and tries to plan for it by building New Towns or adding onto existing cities and towns.

In visiting the New Towns in England, one is impressed not only by the amount that has been built, but by the quality and the way that the British continue to experiment with each New Town, in such areas as housing, transportation, and social planning. The town of Stevenage, for example, has constructed a well-designed, one-story building for the elderly, in the midst of a section bustling with life.

At Basildon, a pedestrian island is surrounded by parking lots. This arrangement provides a pleasant, urban atmosphere for strolling, working, and shopping. The horizontal and vertical thrusts of the buildings are well-balanced and they create an interesting and unified cityscape.

In Runcorn, a New Town near Liverpool, there is a system of independent roads for buses. With sixty public carriers circulating through these direct, traffic-free roads, car travel has been almost eliminated in the town.

The British have also opened new horizons in land reclamation. At least two New Towns are built on land that had been mined or otherwise scarred. The government took the land, filled in the open pits, and built a town on top. This process is costly but sensible, in that it makes otherwise wasted land useful and leaves farmland for farming.

What would Ebenezer Howard think if he came back to the United Kingdom today? First of all, he would see substantial changes in his ideas. The newest New Town, Milton Keynes, for example, will eventually hold 250,000 people, as opposed to Howard's ideal 32,000. Greenbelts surround all the British New Towns and keep them from growing too large, but the expense and shortage of properly located land has meant that none of these greenbelts is as large or dominant as Howard wanted. The variety of housing, most of which is small by American standards, would please Howard because there is a feeling of experimentation, but he might well be baffled because housing styles and materials have changed so much.

He would be pleased that each British New Town is pre-planned, with high value placed on using the land in a full and ecologically sound way. Each New Town is of a predetermined, limited size, and has enough industry to provide jobs for most of its residents. And, while the residents themselves do not own the towns, the government's policy is to subsidize rents to keep them in line with residents' incomes.

Howard would be particularly pleased to see English workers so well housed, and living in such healthy, open environments. Were he alive, he probably would be pushing for faster development in Britain and around the world. But generally, he would be happy with the way his ideas have been accepted and used. All of which, Sir Frederic Osborn contends, demonstrates "the slow contagion of good ideas." That "slow contagion" was to leap the Atlantic Ocean in the early decades of the twentieth century.

# Chapter 4 The Radburn Idea

In recent years, visitors from all over the world have come to see and marvel at the British New Towns. One visitor who came in the early days, however, before it was fashionable, was a young American architect named Clarence Stein. When he arrived in 1920, Letchworth was the only New Town worth seeing. But that was enough to spark his imagination.

He returned determined to build the first American New Town. Radburn, New Jersey was to be the result, and it is still a landmark of New Town building. Not only is it the direct link between Howard's Garden Cities and the American New Town movement, but it is also a dynamic and innovative step forward in New Town planning. In crossing the Atlantic, Howard's ideas were expanded and charged with new life. Elements of the Radburn idea are still being copied in places as distant and diverse as Sweden, Japan, Israel, Brazil, and India.

Clarence Stein, according to his friend and associate Lewis Mumford, was a "rare combination of artist and organizer; a man of fine taste, delicate discrimination, and a background of adequate means that gave him wide opportunities." He was the central magnet and dynamic figure at the center of the New Town movement, as it began in America.

As a young man, Clarence Stein appears to have been drawn to architecture and, at the same time, repelled by the way it was practiced in America. In 1902, he enrolled at Columbia University to study architecture, but left after a year. He then went to Paris to work as an interior decorator, only to decide to try architecture again. This time he enrolled at the École des Beaux Arts in Paris. He graduated in 1911 and returned to the United States to begin a seven year stint with a conventional firm of architects in New York City.

Like Howard, Stein became increasingly concerned with the crowded and unlivable conditions he found in the city. This impulse was reinforced, during his seven years in New York, by association with and by the example of Dr. John Lovejoy Elliott, a leader of the Ethical Culture Society. Dr. Elliott was involved with one of the first public housing projects in New York and was also active in the broader issue of making American society responsive to the problems of the poor. Stein came under his influence and became increasingly involved with what he called "social architecture," or the use of architecture to serve social needs, such as providing inexpensive housing in healthy surroundings. At the end of World War I, Stein left his routine job and began to look for a task with more constructive social meaning.

In 1919, Governor Alfred E. Smith appointed a reconstruction committee for New York and Stein volunteered to be secretary of its housing committee. The job did two things for Stein: It gave him a more precise picture of the housing problems in New York, and it induced him to go abroad to look for useful programs and ideas. In the course of his travels, he made his visit to Letchworth. He also had the opportunity to talk with Ebenezer Howard and Raymond Unwin. He returned to America a disciple of these men and a follower of the Garden City movement.

The particular problem to which Stein addressed himself was the high cost and inadequate supply of good housing in the New York area, particularly for workers. This problem reached acute proportions during the post-World War I period. The price of housing always increases when it is in short supply and people are bidding against each other for every available house or apartment. The fact that rents rose by almost eighty-five percent in all major American cities between 1914 and 1924 gives an indication of just how great the shortage was. Even more discouraging was the fact that new housing was not being built.

The explanation for this extraordinary situation was simple. As the report of Stein's reconstruction committee explained, it was "economically impossible for many years past to provide a large part of the population of this State with decent homes according to American standards of living. Decent homes and wholesome environments in which to bring up children cost more than most workers can afford."

What was to be done? One could ask the government to step in and subsidize housing and provide new initiatives for building it. Or one could come up with a new, more economical way to build good housing, so that a developer or builder could make a profit and also fill a need. This latter method is, of course, the more difficult; but it is the one that would lead to the quickest solution and would result, in the end, in good housing that would take a smaller portion of everyone's paycheck. This was Stein's approach.

In 1920, soon after his return from England, Clarence Stein met with Alexander Bing, a successful New York real estate developer who specialized in apartments and skyscrapers. Bing, a member of the socially sensitive Ethical Culture Society, was looking for something to do that would be of social benefit. He felt that he could be most useful if he were involved in a project that utilized his knowledge and abilities. "I suggested the building of a Garden City," Stein recalls, and "that is how it started."

That is how, at any rate, the City Housing Corporation started. This corporation, like the ones that Howard had used to finance the building of Letchworth and Welwyn, was a strictly limited dividends company. This means that the investors in the company could receive no more than a six percent return on their investment. The purpose of this corporation was to raise capital and handle the other financial aspects of building a Garden City or New Town. First, however, Stein and Bing decided to try something on a smaller scale, so, in 1924, the City Housing Corporation purchased seventy-seven acres of land near Long Island City in the Queens section of New York City, directly across the East River from midtown Manhattan.

On this site, Stein and his architectural partner Henry Wright proposed to build a housing development. This moderate-size project, they hoped, would give them a chance to test ideas, make experiments, and generally prepare themselves for more important ventures. The basic plan for Sunnyside involved placing the housing units (mostly two and three story brick apartments or single and double family houses) attractively around the perimeter of each block. The variety in the height and bulk of the housing, Stein and Wright believed, would create a pleasant visual effect, although the individual buildings, for economy's sake, would almost all be rectangular. The middle of the block was to be left vacant and would serve as an enclave where people could have private gardens and a small common park.

Just two months after the land was purchased, well before all the plans for the site were drawn, the building began. More important, it continued uninterrupted and at a rapid pace throughout the next four years, and this continuity and speed as much as anything else made the project successful.

The housing shortage that Stein and Bing were so concerned about proved an additional advantage in the economics of this project. As soon as a housing unit was completed, people bought homes and moved in. Though houses were sold at cost, and all the building efficiency therefore directly benefited the buyers, Bing sold a portion of the land at considerable financial advantage. Thus, by 1928, the City Housing Corporation could happily report that Sunnyside was a financial success. More than that, it was an attractive, residential community, inhabited overwhelmingly by nonprofessional workers, and located just fifteen minutes by rapid transit from midtown Manhattan.

In 1928, Sunnyside was producing surplus money that the City Housing Corporation could invest in a new venture. This situa-

Sunnyside—an experiment in housing.

tion suited Stein and his colleagues perfectly. Sunnyside was never more than a preliminary step in their minds, and now they were eager to begin work on something bigger and more in-novative. Their goal, as they approached their second project, was to create a "new urban structure," according to Stein, "best suited to the satisfaction of human and biological needs."

Radburn was to be a New Town embodying all of Howard's basic tenets of limited size, advance planning, a proper balance of homes and industry, and an encircling greenbelt. But, in draw-ing up a master plan for Radburn, Wright and Stein were con-cerned about three specific problems that Howard either had not solved or had solved only in part. The first was the high cost and inadequate supply of housing. Second, the planners were concerned about the automobile's disruptive and destructive effect on urban living. Radburn must, they felt, find a solution to the problem of how to live with the auto or, rather, how to live in spite of it. Last, they wanted Radburn to become a community, not simply a pleasant physical environment. "How can we plan," they asked, "so that people have a feeling of neighborliness and a wider field of acquaintanceship?"

On all three points, Howard's ideas were useful. His economic scheme, particularly as it involved buying land at low, rural prices, was important to Stein's belief that he could keep down the cost of housing. Also basic to Stein's hopes of creating a com-munity were Howard's ideas about wards or neighborhoods (so ingeniously put into practice by Raymond Unwin at Letchworth) and Howard's insistence on having people both live and work in the town. But Stein and his associates were far too creative to

wish merely to transplant and duplicate the Garden Cities they
had seen in England.

Inspiration for a new way to build a New Town came in 1928.
Herbert Emmerich, the general manager at Sunnyside, came to
one of the Radburn planning sessions with a schematic sketch
of a superblock indented with dead end streets. Emmerich's
superblock was much larger than an ordinary city block. This
extra size created all kinds of possibilities, such as keeping the
center of the block as common parkland.

The superblocks that were planned for Radburn were to be
thirty-five to fifty acres in size, about eight to ten times the size
of a New York City block. The interior section of each superblock was to be left as parkland, free of both traffic and buildings.
A main road was to run around the perimeter with dead end
streets (cul-de-sacs) branching off. Clustered around each cul-
de-sac were the houses. This particular arrangement of homes
would avoid the ugliness of straight, monotonous rows, and would
mean that each house could face the common parkland and could
also be part of a cluster of other houses.

One of the results of the superblock scheme is that the houses
must be built on very small lots if the housing density of the
whole superblock is to be as high as it is in typical developments.
At Radburn, however, the planners wanted to build at an even
higher density, in order to have large areas of common parkland.
Would people suffer from a lack of privacy? Would they feel
cramped? Would they value these houses as much as other
houses with more individual, private property?

The Radburn planners thought that they could use the unique

structure of the superblock to overcome all these problems, including the last one. The houses could all be set at angles so that no two faced each other directly. A person looking out his window would look past, not at his neighbor's house; this would increase the feeling of privacy. The real key to the superblock, however, was to utilize all the open space and common land in the middle. The Radburn planners extended the central greenery so that it came right to everyone's house. Then they proposed "turning the house around," so that the living room faced the open space out back. Thus, sitting in the living room of a Radburn house, a person looks out at trees and parkland, and is hardly conscious that there are neighbors at all.

The key economic advantage of the superblock is the amount of money that is saved because the street area and the length of the utility lines can be reduced by twenty-five percent. Grading, leveling, and paving a street is enormously expensive, especially compared with the cost of converting open land into a park. The superblock cuts out a number of cross streets, leaving in their stead well-located parkland. The short dead end streets reduce the noise, the speed, and the amount of traffic near the houses.

The real stroke of genius in the planning of Radburn came in using the superblock to make the car less necessary. What is a better form of transportation than car travel, the planners asked? Their answer, at least for travel in town, was walking. It is healthier and cheaper, and avoids the frustrations of parking and repairs. For the community as a whole, it means a cleaner, quieter atmosphere, and more interaction between neighbors.

At Radburn, Stein and Wright elevated the walker to equal

status with the car driver. They built two completely independent traffic systems: one for cars and one for people on foot. This meant building walkways through the central park away from the roads. The system ran conveniently close to every house, providing the residents with a direct foot path from every point in Radburn to every other point.

The real beauty of this plan was that the independent walkway system was designed to connect the common parkland of one superblock with the common parkland of another. This meant that a person could walk to a shop, to church, to school, to work, or to a friend's home, and spend almost all of his time walking in pleasant, natural surroundings. Where it became necessary to cross the roads running around the perimeter of each superblock, the walkers could use a series of tunnels and bridges. A person would not have to interrupt his walk to cross a street, and, even more important, Radburn would be a much safer place for children.

With all of these exciting plans circulating through the planners' minds, the City Housing Corporation finally settled on a site for the project. In 1929, it purchased a large tract of rural land in Fair Lawn, New Jersey. The site was almost entirely farmland and had the additional advantage of being near the main route leading to the Hudson River's George Washington Bridge, then under construction.

The initial outlines of the Radburn master plan show three neighborhoods, each consisting of at least three residential superblocks and each centered on an elementary school. From the school to the outskirts of each neighborhood was a maximum of

Separating people from cars, a basic New Town concept.

a half mile in any direction. On the hill where the outskirts of the three neighborhoods came together, Wright and Stein planned to build a community center and a high school.

Another section of the Radburn site was marked off as a downtown area with plans for a regional shopping center and a regional theater. The planners also marked off an area conveniently close to both a state highway and a railroad line for industry. Unfortunately, land for a greenbelt could not be purchased. In Britain, so long as land is used for agriculture or open space, purchase rates are low. In the United States, the system of taxing land at its highest potential value makes greenbelt land prohibitively expensive.

As at Sunnyside, there was not enough time to work out the details of Radburn's master plan before starting to build. Every effort was made to get the actual construction under way. Several superblocks were laid out and foundations were poured almost immediately after the purchase. Streets, parks, and utility lines were timed so that they were completed at exactly the same time as the houses. The Sunnyside experience was paying off handsomely.

The first problem the City Housing Corporation faced was one that they had recognized in advance. By wishing to start from scratch, they had gone outside the web of services and utility lines of any major city. Instead of merely adding to the municipal services of a city, as had been done at Sunnyside, Radburn had to build its own sewage disposal plants and set down large utility lines.

The real problem facing Radburn, however, was outside the

realm of city planning and construction. Less then six months after the first residents moved into the unfinished town in 1929, the stock market crashed. At first, Radburn was unaffected and the corporation continued to build houses. But slowly the economic depression forced its way into Radburn.

The first casualty was industry. The Radburn developers counted on getting new industries or expansion-minded older companies to buy sites and build factories and offices in Radburn. But, with world trade at a standstill and money in short supply, industrial expansion had ceased and businesses were struggling simply to stay open.

Then came the problem of credit. The City Housing Corporation needed large sums of money in order to build quickly and efficiently. As the Depression came on, however, credit dried up, and soon there was no money with which to continue building. Each year fewer and fewer houses were built, until in 1933 only twelve new homes were started. Even in the best of times, this slow development could not yield enough income to pay the large debt on the land.

Finally, the housing market collapsed. A great many people needed good housing, but most of them were out of work and could not afford to pay even a modest rent. In addition, some of the people living in Radburn lost their jobs and had to give up their houses. Where was the money to come from to pay off the large debt for the purchase and development of the land at Radburn? No one knew the answer.

In 1936 the City Housing Corporation went into bankruptcy. Except for the parks and open spaces, the undeveloped land—

the greenbelt, the industrial area, the downtown, and even most of the residential land—was sold. All that remained were two superblocks and other fragments of an heroic undertaking.

Radburn's failure to become a New Town is, it seems, one of the significant tragedies that occurred during the Depression. If the experiment had been successful, its example might have encouraged developers during the 1940s and 1950s to build something better than the monotonous land-gobbling suburbs. In the plan for Radburn there was an originality, a perceptiveness, and a boldness that might have caught on. Instead of suburban sprawl, we might have built hundreds of New Towns that would have significantly reduced our present urban and environmental crises.

In one way, however, Radburn was not a failure. The Depression kept it from becoming a New Town, but enough was built to demonstrate the Radburn idea. "The two superblocks that were built, and in which people have lived happily," Clarence Stein claims, "have demonstrated the essentials of the new form of city that is increasingly accepted as the basis for planning urban, residential areas in Europe and America."

Radburn today is still unusual in many ways. The physical design, which can only be appreciated on foot, gives one a sense of great spaciousness and openness. The superblocks built during the 1930s contain 677 family houses and 100 apartment units. These superblocks are connected by a tunnel and give a feeling for what the town might have been, had it been completed.

Radburn houses about 2,500 people, approximately one tenth

of the original Garden City projection. In essence, therefore, Radburn is a large housing development. Nevertheless, it has enormous significance for New Town planners because a number of important concepts have been tried out there. The fact that residents have found Radburn a good place to live means, for example, that people can live harmoniously on small plots close together. We do not need anywhere near a quarter of an acre of land between houses, Radburn has demonstrated, in order to have a quiet, friendly neighborhood.

Radburn today is relentlessly middle class. The Radburn ideal of low cost housing for workers has failed, but, interestingly, the reason is market pressure and not building costs. What happened in Radburn, and what presents a real dilemma for New Town planners everywhere, is that houses that originally sold at prices workers could afford simply increased in market price. When the original owners came to resell their houses, they found the houses could be sold for a much higher price than the owners had paid. Thus, with each resale, the cost of housing in Radburn has gone up and up, and the middle class has taken over.

The age mix of people living in Radburn has changed significantly during the last forty years. New Towns have traditionally started as colonies of the young, and Radburn was no exception. Today, however, Radburn boasts a far more diversified age range than is found in most suburbs. Many of the original inhabitants, now retired, are still around, but the gradual turnover of people has meant that they now live side by side with young married couples, a core of middle-aged people, and lots of children.

More important, Radburn, even as a middle class community,

has maintained an economic diversity that is far greater than most places in our increasingly homogenized society. Here a person may live in a house costing a third or two thirds less than his neighbor's. The cheapest house sold in Radburn during the early seventies, for example, went for $21,000, and nearby the most expensive one sold for $68,000. There is also an apartment complex integrated into one of the superblocks, all of which indicates that a well planned New Town can gracefully and happily accommodate people with a wide range of incomes.

Physical planning, however, is not all that makes Radburn work. The architects and planners were well aware that a physical environment is only the first step in creating a satisfying place to live. The City Housing Corporation, therefore, went far beyond superblocks and cul-de-sacs, and established an organization of residents called the Radburn Association.

This association is essentially a service organization, paid for by the residents of Radburn, that attempts to meet their needs and problems. Each person who buys a house or rents an apartment in Radburn automatically becomes a member of this association and pays a yearly fee based on the value of his or her property. The Radburn Citizen's Association, in turn, takes care of the common parkland, the tennis courts, the swimming pools, and the other shared facilities. Its main function, however, is to serve the human needs of the residents, whether this means organizing a summer program for youngsters, a winter basketball league, or adult classes and discussion groups.

Radburn has some distinct limitations. Not only does it lack industry and appropriate size, but, being largely middle class, it lacks the excitement and diversity of life styles that make an urban area a rich and rewarding place to live. People seem to walk a good deal there, but the car is still the predominant mode of transportation. The single detached house is also the predominant residential unit, which leads to the conclusion that even a completed Radburn would have made some important concessions to traditional American living patterns. Nevertheless, Radburn still retains a sense of pride and distinctiveness.

Chapter **5** The Government Towns

Though people live comfortably in Radburn today, America's first experimental New Town exists as a fragment of the dream that created it. Furthermore, the depression years that shattered Radburn were in no way conducive to the creation of other New Towns. Private enterprise was struggling to avoid a complete breakdown. No company could afford the risks of a venture like Radburn. In addition, the big problem was no longer housing workers, but housing the unemployed. Masses of people needed shelter, but what private company could afford to build homes for people who could not pay rent?

Some of the destitute were driven to construct their own shelters and to build their own "towns" on bits of vacant city land. Constructed of scraps of metal, tin cans, and packing boxes, these ramshackle clusters of hovels were called Hoovervilles, after the president who was in office during this tragic era. One of the shantytowns sprang up in the nation's capital itself. The plight of the homeless was held up to official and public view in a most dramatic fashion.

In 1933, when the Hoovervilles were a small but vivid illustration of the country's plight, Franklin D. Roosevelt, with his
pledge of a New Deal, was swept into the presidency. He promised to "forge new tools for a new role of government in a
democracy—a role of new responsibility for new needs and increased responsibility for old needs, long neglected."

In 1935 Congress passed the Emergency Relief Appropriations
Act and the National Industrial Recovery Act. These measures
opened the way for direct government action in dealing with
such problems as unemployment and the shortage of housing.

Rexford Guy Tugwell, one of Roosevelt's "brain trusters," was
selected as head of the newly created Resettlement Administration. He attacked the gigantic problems of the housing shortage
in a number of ways. One of the boldest, most controversial, and
most far-reaching of his approaches was the building of the
Greenbelt Towns.

The name "Greenbelt Town" was derived from Ebenezer
Howard's idea of encircling a new community with a girdle of
undeveloped land. Tugwell liked this idea and the greenbelt became a prominent feature in the design of these government
sponsored towns. What was really significant about the Greenbelt
Towns, however, was the government's willingness to become
directly involved in their planning and building, and in seeing to
it that these new communities met pressing human needs in a
creative, life-enhancing way.

The government's goals were a rare and exciting blend of the
practical and the idealistic. Pragmatically, the Greenbelt Towns
were to provide decent housing for families with incomes as low

as $1,250 a year. They were also to provide jobs for the unem-
ployed, some of whom might then become residents. But the
project also aimed to supply more than temporary housing to
meet an emergency. According to the Resettlement Administration, one of the official purposes was to "demonstrate in practice
the soundness of planning and operating towns according to
certain Garden City principles." Rather than create shoddy structures destined for demolition in more prosperous times, the
Greenbelt Towns were to be innovatively planned communities
that could serve as permanent examples for future city planners.

Though the United States government was behind this project, the Greenbelt Towns were only a small part of the government's strategy for economic recovery. Thus, funds were severely
limited. Government officials did not view the enterprise as an
ongoing financial obligation, but rather as an investment that
should eventually pay for itself. Considering, therefore, how inexpensive the housing would have to be in order to minimize the
debt, the project became, in large part, a test of how cheaply
sturdy housing could be built when organized along Garden City
lines.

Next came the questions of how many towns to build and
where to locate them. Four were seriously considered. Tugwell
and his associates decided to place the new communities close to
big cities where most of the population growth was taking place.

The architects, planners, and technicians who were to create
the Greenbelt Towns were divided into teams, each responsible
for a single town. This system was used so that every community
would become a distinct experiment, utilizing new ideas and

hitherto untried approaches. As a result, each of the towns eventually emerged with a unique individuality.

The first site selected was in Maryland, thirteen miles from Washington, D.C., and the town created on this tract was named Greenbelt. The other new communities were Greendale, Wisconsin, seven miles from the business center of Milwaukee, and Greenhills, Ohio, five miles north of Cincinnati. The fourth town, Greenbrook, New Jersey, never got past the drawing board because of challenges by local residents and a federal court ruling that held this an unconstitutional use of federal funds. Tugwell declared, "O.K., it's unconstitutional in New Jersey," and went ahead with the others.

The three Greenbelt Towns that finally took form did not attract industry and therefore were never complete New Towns in Ebenezer Howard's sense of the term. However, they are all in existence today and continue to reflect the openness and careful use of land that makes a pleasant environment for living.

Greenbelt, Maryland became a great showpiece of Garden City planning. In addition, it developed the Radburn idea of superblocks, with clustering of housing, shared greenery, and separation of traffic, more fully than any of the other towns, and in some ways more than Radburn itself. Thus, rather than tell the story of the three towns, we will concentrate on Greenbelt.

Greenbelt was planned and designed to fit harmoniously into the contours of the open countryside. The site was a curved plateau, a few miles north of Washington. Greenbelt rose on the natural tableland, taking the shape of a graceful crescent, in a vast setting of greenery.

Five superblocks—with their separation of traffic, their central greens, and shaded walkways—were laid out, and the first homes, 885 in number, were built between 1935 and 1937. The middle of the crescent was the focus for communal activity. The shopping center was designed as a modern version of the medieval market square from which all vehicular traffic was banned.

Around this quiet square were grouped the buildings needed for carrying out the various functions of community life—education, government, and recreation. The center, within easy walking distance of each house, became the informal gathering place of the residents. The creation of this multipurpose town center was, in the eyes of Clarence Stein, "the most important forward step made at Greenbelt toward the evolution of New Towns that fit the special problems of these times."

The first inhabitants moved into their well-built, rectangular, attached houses in the fall of 1937 and the summer of 1938. The housing was in such demand that people had to apply well in advance. Preference was given to poorly housed families whose incomes were limited but who could still afford home rentals of about twenty-two to forty-six dollars per month.

The innovative planning, the unusual appearance, and the New Town idea gave many of the people arriving at Greenbelt the feeling of being pioneers. In the first issue of the *Cooperator*, the town's weekly journal, a newly settled resident expressed this sentiment in a vivid way:

We are pioneers—of a new way of living. . . . This project has given most of us an opportunity we'd never anticipated. We are in the process of creating homes! Our families and our children will live under laws of our own making. Only in our fondest and most youthful dreams have we imagined such a chance. What will we make of it?

What they made of it is a long and sometimes turbulent story. The early days brought controversy and attack.

There was the question of architecture. Some heralded the economic achievement: building durable housing in an open, green environment, at unbelievably low cost. Others were sharply critical of the barracks-like three family homes, Greenbelt's predominant type of housing.

Even more controversial was the idea, developed at Radburn, of having the front of the house face the greenery instead of the street. The *Denver Post*, for example, described Greenbelt as "a topsy-turvy town where no one knows whether they are approaching a front or a back door."

Partly because of the general suspicion of "big government," the rumor spread that the people of Greenbelt were being regimented through federal rules and regulations. One large real estate and rental agency, when asked to supply a reference for a person who had applied for housing in Greenbelt, wrote back, "It is not the policy of this office to furnish information for these government projects which it is felt are unAmerican and tend to Communism."

Taking in stride the criticism of their new community, the pioneers of Greenbelt moved forward to develop their own intensive civic life. The New Town atmosphere was conducive to the testing of experimental ideas. One of those ideas resulted in the organization of all the commercial enterprises on a consumer-cooperative basis. When this experiment succeeded, other cooperatives were quick to follow: the newspaper, the credit union, the nursery school, the health association. In fact, the idea of cooperatives became so infectious that, in the fall of 1937, the elementary school children started a junior cooperative for such items as candy, pencils, and paper.

Several events, national in scope, had major effects on the history of Greenbelt. The first was World War II, with its attendant and aggravated housing shortage. In 1941, one thousand new dwelling units were built for defense workers. Funds were so severely limited that the considerations of aesthetics and even of safety were to some degree sacrificed.

The most crucial happening, however, of Greenbelt's postwar history was the complete withdrawal of the federal government from the scene in 1949. The Greenbelt Towns were established as an emergency measure during the depression years. By 1949 there was an economic boom in the country. That the towns represented more than a makeshift response to a crisis, that they were, in fact, unusual experiments in new ways of community living, did not weigh in the final balance. Thus, when the initial appropriations had been spent, the federal government decided to wash its hands of the Greenbelt Towns. Congress subsequently passed a law for their disposition.

Greenbelters were unwilling to see their towns and their dreams sold to the highest bidder. Each town handled the situation in its own way.

In Maryland, the Greenbelt residents, banding together in a cooperative homeowners' corporation, purchased their homes and land from the government's Public Housing Administration. Subsequently, the PHA deeded to the city the recreational areas, public buildings, and streets. An important part of the greenbelt itself was saved when the government made the 1,400 acres south of the town into a national park.

The opening of a major parkway between Washington and Baltimore, with an exit at Greenbelt, and the placing of a national center for space research within a stone's throw, made the Greenbelt area an increasingly desirable place for living.

As population pressure mounted, land prices started to skyrocket. Developers were quick to snatch up property within the precincts of the city of Greenbelt, and to put up new subdivisions. But these did not follow garden city principles. They were simply attractive, modern, single family suburban developments for people of comfortable means—hardly the original New Town idea.

Nevertheless, the Garden City concept, though fragmented, is still very much alive. In the old section of Greenbelt, the housing built in the late 1930s and early 1940s still has a distinctiveness and style of its own. There are the groups of two story multiple dwelling units clustered around cul-de-sacs. The lack of frills on these plain, rectangular buildings indicates how cost-conscious the planners were. This old part of Greenbelt is unusually open and spacious, with large green areas for relaxing or playing, and nearby woods for exploring. The churches, schools, and homes are well-integrated into the open space and woodland.

Though today's Greenbelt Towns are little more than pleasant suburbs, that "little more" represents an important link in a chain. First came the British New Towns, then Radburn, then the Greenbelt Towns, then a few other Garden City developments that were extensions of cities, and next, America's *new* New Towns. Historically, it took another quarter century before the preplanning of an entire community along Garden City lines was to be tried again.

Chapter **6** Reston: Rebirth of the New Town Idea

In the rolling Virginia countryside about thirty miles west of Washington, D.C., an elegant apartment tower suddenly comes into view. Heron House, as this fifteen story brick building is called, signals the approach to the New Town of Reston. Rising high above the trees and houses, it is the first sign of urban life in this country setting.

Lake Anne Village Center, where pedestrian traffic is the only kind permitted, is a good starting point for a visit. Lake Anne Center has received more praise for its handsome architecture and overall design then any complex of buildings and plazas in any New Town in America. Particularly attractive is the graceful horseshoe of shops and apartments at the perimeter of the central plaza. But it is the whole conception—the openness of the lake balancing the enclosed buildings, the horizontal thrust of the townhouses interacting with the soaring reach of Heron House—that makes Lake Anne Center so appealing. In fact, the center is a remarkable testimony to what a creative group of architects can do when designing a whole urban complex from scratch.

The buildings do more than look well and fit attractively together. The plazas handle crowds nicely, whether they consist of shoppers or large gatherings for outdoor concerts and speeches. In addition, walking around between the townhouses, offices, churches, day care center, tennis courts, swimming pools and golf courses, one notices that it is very convenient to go from place to place on foot. Yet there is plenty of open space and never a sense of overcrowding.

The man-made lake that gives this village center its name serves a number of functions. First, of course, is the simple aesthetic aspect. It is a beautiful, oblong lake, with a spectacular water fountain in the middle. In summer, it is also a place for boats, fishermen, and even an occasional swimmer. But, in addition, Lake Anne is connected to the air conditioning plant that services this part of Reston and the sprinkling system on the golf course. Thus, by careful planning, Lake Anne has been created to fulfill several needs efficiently.

All of Reston, but especially Lake Anne Center, makes you feel that you have never before been in such a place. All the buildings have been completed in the last ten years, and their stark and simple forms are like contemporary sculpture. Another reason Reston seems unusual is the accentuation of certain features, such as the number of townhouses. They constitute more than two thirds of the housing in Reston.

Small touches contribute their share to the Reston atmosphere. Along some promenades and walkways, for example, are an assortment of decorative concrete sculptures, which also serve as playthings for children to climb on. Even the bridges on the walk-

Lake Anne, Reston—blending city and country.

way system have a flair, in the way they arch over canals and roadways.

The person chiefly responsible for the creation of Reston, and for many of its distinguishing features, is Robert E. Simon, Jr. His personality is indelibly etched into this town, from its name (derived from his initials and the English "ton," meaning town) to its goals and community programs. Reston has been called Simon's "brainchild" and his "fiefdom." Even his critics agree that, without Simon, Reston would never have come into existence.

Robert Simon is thoughtful and articulate, and though he rarely raises his voice, one senses that he is a person of strong opinions and deep convictions. Simon's route to Reston is an interesting one. It begins with his father, who was on the Board of Directors of the City Housing Corporation, the agency responsible for Radburn, when Robert, Jr. was a teenager. Thus, long before Reston became a possibility, Simon was well-acquainted with the New Town movement from Ebenezer Howard to Radburn and the Greenbelt Towns.

In 1961, Robert Simon's family business sold its largest piece of real estate, Carnegie Hall in New York City. In looking for a way to invest the money, Simon stumbled on a large land deal. He bought 6,750 acres (to which he later added 650 acres) in northern Virginia.

Simon's motivation for building a New Town was partially to make money, but it was also to create a new and better living environment. Simon deplored the amount of land wasted in a typical suburban development. "The front lawn of a house," he explained, "is neither public nor private." It is private in that it belongs to the house, so that no one but the homeowner can use it; but since it usually adjoins a street and is in full public view, it is rarely used. The side lawn, too, is usually wasted, Simon contended, because its narrow shape tends to make it little more than a passageway. Even the back lawn, Simon felt, is not functionally sound: it is "larger than needed for sunbathing, but smaller than needed for baseball or tennis." If Reston were built along typical suburban lines on quarter acre lots, he explained, its 7,400 acres would provide housing, but little else, for some 75,000 people.

Simon wanted to build something that had more vitality than a residential suburb. On this same 7,400 acres, Simon insisted, he could build a New Town that would provide its residents with nearby employment, a full range of educational and cultural facilities, and a large amount of useable open space—and still house 75,000 people. The secret was to build attached townhouses instead of detached houses, and to clump them together in small clusters. By planning the whole town in advance, this clustering could be done functionally and attractively, providing plenty of shared open land around each cluster.

One of the first people Simon consulted and engaged was an architect named Julian Whittlesey. Whittlesey, as a young architect, had helped Clarence Stein and Henry Wright design Radburn. He and his firm created an entirely different master plan for Reston, but the carryover from Radburn is evident. Two of the most obvious borrowings are the clustering of houses around open space and the use of underpasses and overpasses to separate pedestrian and automobile traffic.

Experts in everything from energy to community associations were hired in 1961, to aid in the planning of Reston. The master plan that emerged is based on high density, medium density, and low density residential areas. A high density area would be one that had a large number of townhouses and garden apartments, or even an apartment building, and would be designed to house an average of sixty people per acre. A medium density area would be much more open, averaging only fourteen people per acre, which would mean only three or four houses to the acre. Low density areas would provide housing for an average of just under four people per acre.

The amount of acreage of high density, low density, and medium density housing in Reston was not an arbitrary decision by the planners. The sewage system and utility lines in Fairfax County—the county in which Reston is located—have a capacity that prohibits an overall density of more than thirteen persons per gross residential acre. This figure is high by ordinary suburban standards.

Most suburbs and subdivisions are built with a like number of houses per acre of land, and zoning laws are written accordingly. Simon's desire to vary his zones of residential housing so that one acre might hold one or two houses, and another have eight or ten townhouses or even an apartment building, was a radical departure in the field of urban planning. He argued that, for a large entity like Reston, he should be regulated only by an overall average density, rather than by acre-by-acre restrictions. This new approach was one of Simon's most significant contributions to New Town planning in America.

Thinking of housing in terms of a particular number of people for an area of ten or twenty connected acres allowed the planners great flexibility. Even in a high density area, they might build a couple of apartment buildings and place a park or a group of tennis courts between them. Above all, the planners attempted to make each area attractive and to keep even the highest density areas from being denied open recreational land. Instead of following the usual pattern, which is to surround high density housing with medium and then low density housing in bull's eye fashion, the Reston planners created a high density sinew, which winds this way and that through the whole estate and is never the center of a large boxed-in area. William Conklin, one of the chief planners, cited the statistic that, in our country, twenty percent of all trips by car are taken to get to recreational areas. Energy crisis or no, the people of Reston find recreation close at hand.

In order to convince the Fairfax County Board to accept his ideas, Simon rented an office across the street from the county offices, so that he could work with the board every step of the way and not have to present his plans to them full-blown.

Theoretically, it should not have been too difficult to sell Fairfax County on a New Town that promised to be physically attractive, ecologically sound, and financially beneficial to the county. Still, Reston was something out of the ordinary, a project that went against all the usual zoning regulations. Fairfax County was, therefore, skeptical and cautious about granting Simon the zoning change he wanted and the O.K. to go ahead with Reston. In June, 1962, however, the Board of Supervisors met and adopted into law Residential Planned Community Zoning, which meant, essentially, an acceptance of the Reston master plan. Gulf Oil advanced the mortgage money to Simon early in 1963 and Reston began to rise.

Reston, unlike Radburn, was born into an era of prosperity and hope. The years between 1961 and 1963 found the country in a bouyant, optimistic mood.

The first people who moved into Reston, in late 1964, were young and well-educated. They belonged to all sorts of ethnic and racial groups and, by and large, shared the optimism of the country and the belief that America was moving into an era that would see the end of racial and ethnic hatred.

These first inhabitants were also filled with a pioneer spirit, as were the people who settled in Letchworth, Radburn, and Greenbelt. They were determined to make Reston something better than the suburbs and cities from which they came. Innumerable organizations and clubs sprang up. There was an aura of adventure about this New Town that brought people together in camaraderie and friendship.

Today Reston has become a more conventional community. "Reston offers all the open space and recreational facilities one goes away on vacation for," one resident remarked, which sounded uncomfortably like an advanced form of an argument for moving to the suburbs. This impression was reinforced by a high school student who commented that "Reston today is a place for $10,000 to $20,000-a-year people who want to pretend they are more than that."

While some of the initial excitement has gone out of the Reston experiment, its residents have not yet become typical suburbanites. There are still, for example, an incredible number of organizations and clubs with large memberships. Reston still has its cluster associations and homeowners association that play an active role not only in maintaining community facilities, but in instituting useful programs. And the *Reston Times,* the community's excellent newspaper, gives evidence that the town is not stagnating. In one of its 1973 issues, there are articles about a course in landscape architecture sponsored by the Reston Nature Center, and another adult course on Urban Economy, given at the Virginia Tech Campus in Reston by a team of specialists from the Urban Institute in Washington. This indicates that the residents continue to be stimulated by their New Town, and that they are still interested in the larger implications of urban development.

Two organizations at Reston, Common Ground and the Nature Center, demonstrate innovative ways of filling some of the voids that can occur in a New Town. These are the two organizations of which Restonians seem proudest.

Common Ground owes its existence and success to a dynamic Protestant minister named Embry Rucker, who came to Reston in its early days and decided that Reston did not need another church. What Reston needed badly was a place where its teenagers could relax and socialize. He helped set up a coffee house in Lake Anne Center, and put his office in a spot where people who wanted to could informally walk in and talk with him.

Teenagers accepted the place and volunteered to work behind

the counter, serving food and drinks. And so, as Rucker hoped, the place really became theirs. Common Ground was soon paying its own expenses. Rucker raised money from his congregation and from voluntary contributions and expanded his endeavors. The Common Ground Foundation is responsible for such things as the free community bus, the day-care center, a sitter-referral service, a nursing service, a nursery school, a youth-employment service, and emergency help.

Common Ground's coffers do not overflow with money, but it has maintained a very firm policy about not compromising its ideals in order to obtain large contributions. Its support comes from small contributions, from people in the community who like what Common Ground is doing.

In contrast with Common Ground, the Nature Center does not need to go directly to the Reston residents for contributions. It was instituted by the developer, and today it is under the auspices of the Reston Homeowners Association. A long-time science teacher, Vernon Walker, was recruited to Reston by Robert Simon and instructed to set up an organization that would enable residents to get involved with and take advantage of their environment.

"The Nature Center," according to Vernon Walker, "is really a program, not a place." Knowing only too well the limitations of a classroom, especially for educating people about the outdoors, Mr. Walker spends little time on displays and lectures, and instead devotes most of his instructional time to walks and other activities where experience can teach far more than his words.

Vernon Walker gives his attention to adults almost as much

as to children. One weekend, for example, he assembled a group of volunteers who mulched and planted a river bank under his direction. "It saves money," he explained, "but it also gives the participants an experience and a sense of identification with the land."

The Nature Center has Ranger Rick and Junior Trailblazer clubs for youngsters, but perhaps its most interesting program is the one for teenagers. This program includes paid jobs: outlining the boundaries of the open land, painting swimming pool bottoms, and building tot lots.

The Nature Center has worked because it has taken a positive and often sophisticated approach toward the Reston environment. In addition to traditional activities such as nature walks, the center embarks on imaginative undertakings such as trying to cultivate blueberries and planting vegetation that will attract a greater variety of wildlife. *American Forests* magazine, in an article about the Nature Center, summed up its place in Reston in this way: "The common-land planning of Reston and the educational guidance offered by the Nature Center for the use and care of this land present a unique opportunity for one community to have a better urban environment."

Admirable as both the Nature Center and Common Ground are, they don't solve completely a persistent problem. In our society teenagers tend to be skeptical of established programs, but they often do not know where else to turn. For those who do not get involved in a particular hobby or program, long stretches of time during adolescence can be lonely and boring. This feeling was expressed by a couple of Reston teenagers sitting in the local drug store, who, to the question of how they liked Reston, answered, "It's pretty, but there's nothing to do."

New Town developers argue that New Towns have more facilities—swimming pools, teen centers, tennis courts, parks—than any suburb, hence more potential for dealing with the "nothing-to-do" problem. However, the fact is that it is confusing and difficult for young people to move into an unfamiliar environment without any old friends. For all the thoughtful Reston planning that aims at fostering a "sense of belonging," a thirteen- or fourteen-year-old person still has a hard time overcoming his isolation when his family moves to a new place. And for everyone, Reston is a new place.

In trying to evaluate how successful Reston has been in meeting its goals as a New Town, we can begin by looking at the area in which both Radburn and the Greenbelt Towns failed: the ability to attract industry. Reston has two important conventional attractions: nearness to the large Washington market and close access to Dulles International Airport. But what Reston's developers really relied on was that Reston would provide such a good living environment that firms concerned about keeping their employees would locate there. In technology-oriented industries, like computer companies, the ability to attract and keep highly skilled people is an important factor for success.

The data is incomplete, but certainly Reston has done well numerically in attracting research firms and some light industry. It has over fifty business firms and associations, ranging from the

American Newspaper Publishers to Reston Cable TV, Inc. to Schonstedt Instrument Company. Its greatest industrial acquisition, however, came in 1966, when the United States Government decided to build its fifty million dollar headquarters for the United States Geological Survey in Reston. This means not only a large number of jobs, but the kind of jobs that pay enough so that the employees can easily afford to live in the New Town.

The convenience and sense of community that develops when people live where they work is, of course, an essential part of New Town theory and, in this aspect, Reston still has a long way to go. Each morning, approximately 1,700 people board express buses for Washington and, each evening, the roadways to Reston are jammed with cars. Paradoxically, many people also commute to Reston to work in its plants and shops. Still, the developers are hopeful that these patterns will change with time, as more and more residents find jobs in Reston that are as good as the ones they now commute to.

Building a heterogeneous community that would be balanced both racially and economically was as important as bringing industry to Reston. The Reston developers have been adamant about a policy of open housing from the start. Consequently, people who come to Reston expect to find an integrated community, and black families have encountered none of the resistance all too common in their attempts to get into lily-white suburbs.

Reston has also tried to become a community where people with a wide range of incomes live side by side. An apartment complex called Cedar Ridge, which is virtually indistinguishable from the rest of Reston, is occupied by people of low and moderate income. And the 138-unit highrise called Fellowship House provides housing for people over age fifty-five with incomes under $5,400.

There are several other housing units for people with low and moderate incomes, but, unfortunately, the program is nowhere near the ten to fifteen percent which Reston's developers had hoped for. The problem, according to Robert Simon, is that land, land development, and construction costs make it impossible to build low or even moderate income housing that pays for itself. Government subsidies are needed in a project of this kind, and, unless these are made available, new communities like Reston will never be able to house their share of poor people. Today Reston is even failing in many instances to provide housing for its own gardeners, garbage collectors, and postmen.

Reston is now entering a phase of rapid growth. With a present population of 22,000, it should eventually reach its goal of housing 74,000 people. In 1970 a survey showed that sixty-one percent of Reston's adults found it an "excellent" place to live. But Reston's growth has not been without problems. Robert Simon insisted on outstanding architecture and quality building materials. He added embellishments like concrete sculptures, an artificial lake, and a large brick plaza. He felt that unless Reston was outstanding, innovative, and beautiful it would fail.

In 1966 Simon went back to Gulf Oil to try to borrow more money. Gulf decided that too much money had been spent on "frills" and that Reston was in serious financial trouble. In 1967, Gulf, which had over $18,000,000 tied up in Reston, took control of the operation, replacing Simon with its own man.

Whether Reston was on the brink of bankruptcy is still a disputed point. The Gulf people will never build anything as elegant and innovative as Lake Anne Center, but they are trying to stay within the guidelines of Reston's master plan. When the enterprise is complete, in another ten to twenty years, it will still be a New Town, and it will have the important distinction of being the first complete New Town in America.

Even now, in its incomplete state, Reston has accomplished something of historic proportions. It has gotten the New Town idea under way again. Reston started people talking about New Towns and about how they can meet the pressing need for housing in more than a stop-gap, chaotic way.

In recent times, many people and businesses have become increasingly concerned about channeling more resources into enterprises of significant social benefit. James Rouse, president of the Rouse Corporation, is such a person. He is a successful real estate developer and mortgage banker. He is also a man willing to take a risk for something in which he believes. Rouse saw in Reston a project he felt was highly significant, exciting, and creative, so he plunged himself and his company into a New Town venture called Columbia.

Chapter **7** Columbia: Making New Towns Profitable

In October, 1961, James Rouse flew over Howard County, Maryland, in a helicopter. Rouse was interested in building a New Town, and Howard County, a semi-rural area in the corridor between Baltimore and Washington, was an ideal spot. Nothing much came of this scouting mission, however, until six months later, when a 1,039 acre estate was put up for sale. Through a Baltimore real estate firm, Rouse bid on the property and bought it, for just under $600 an acre.

Shortly before the final settlement on this purchase, another 428 acre tract came on the market, and Rouse bought that, through a friend.

Rouse now began to calculate that he would need 12,000 acres of adjoining land to build the kind of New Town he wanted, with an ultimate population of about 100,000 people. The big question was, could he get that much land quickly through this kind of piecemeal buying, and get it at a reasonable price?

Rouse believed that he could, though it would be an unprecedented accomplishment. In order to do it, he knew he would need a big financial backer. So he went to the chairman of Connecticut General Life Insurance Company, Frazier Wilde. "There is no use in our attempting to kid you," Rouse remembers telling Wilde. "There's absolutely no way this can be done unless Connecticut General will put up all the money to buy the land.

"We will manage this enterprise. We will provide funds for its planning. We will invest one million dollars in it. . . . But . . . you have to look at it in these terms: You can't possibly lose money if you invest in the purchase of 12,000 acres of land midway between Baltimore and Washington."

Insurance companies simply do not invest $18 million in risky, unsecured ventures. But Rouse had two things going for him. First, he was able to communicate his vision of what a New Town could be and why it was necessary. Second, he had his own reputation and long-established, mutually profitable association with Connecticut General. "I don't think we would have done it with anyone but Jim," one Connecticut General executive explained after Wilde had made the bold decision to back Rouse and his project. Connecticut General would advance $18 million (later raised to $23 million) to acquire the land for Columbia.

Speed and secrecy were now of the essence to keep land prices from skyrocketing. Rouse and his associates selected a 25,000 acre area in Howard County where they thought they had the best chance to acquire the 12,000 acres they needed, to build the kind of New Town they wanted. Except for three large estates, however, all the land in this part of Howard County was in small parcels, which made the undertaking all the more difficult. Rouse decided on the shotgun approach of buying every parcel he could in the 25,000 acre target zone and worrying later about how they might fit together. Thus began one of the greatest "cloak-and-dagger" land acquisition operations in the history of town building.

Rouse established a group of companies with innocent-sounding names like Potomac Estates, Farmingdale, and Serenity Acres, to buy the land. A variety of real estate agents did the actual negotiations for these companies, and they had no idea that they were all part of a front for the Rouse Company. Additional precautions also had to be taken in handling the vast sums of money from Connecticut General. Accounts were opened in a number of different banks and the money was juggled back and forth so that not even the banks would know how much money Rouse controlled.

After 12,000 acres of farmland in separate parcels had been assembled, Connecticut General and Rouse decided to expand to 15,000 acres and to link the various pieces of property together. In order to do this, however, they had to come to terms with the three large landowners in the region.

After buying out two of these landowners, they encountered great difficulty with the third, a retired sand and gravel tycoon. All the land buying had tipped him off that something big was going on. What he did not know was that he held the property that would some day be downtown Columbia. The price finally agreed to was $3 million or $3,000 an acre—five times what Rouse had paid when he started buying land in Howard County.

The land caper was over. Rouse had assembled 164 farms totaling 15,500 acres, almost one tenth of Howard County. The price was $23 million, an average of $1,450 per acre. He had done it in just nine months.

While the massive land acquisition progressed, rumors spread.

The combined sanitation departments of Baltimore and Washington were going to use the site to convert garbage into a kind of organic peat moss. No, others argued, this was to be a missile site. In October, 1963, James Rouse put an end to the rumors. He announced that he planned to build a New Town there. That was certainly better than a sanitation site, people agreed, but not much.

The reason people reacted so negatively to the idea of a New Town was that they were afraid of an influx of outsiders and what this migration would do to their peaceful, semi-rural county. In fact, just before Rouse's land caper, the people of Howard County had overwhelmingly voted into office three county commissioners who had run on one basic issue—no new growth for Howard County.

"I like Howard County the way it is," was a typical reaction. Columbia would mean "higher taxes, more crowded schools, and housing projects instead of farms," the residents felt. And who could blame them for feeling threatened by the idea of 100,000 new people pouring into their country and tripling its population? If Rouse thought he could get new zoning and build a New Town, they replied, he had something to learn.

Rouse also had something to teach. He and his chief planners went all over Howard County, speaking at luncheons, teas, clubs, and anywhere else they could find an audience. They did not argue that townhouses were more attractive than farms, but that development was coming to Howard County in one form or another. Situated where it was, between the nation's fastest-growing metropolitan area, Washington, D.C., and the ninth-fastest, Baltimore, Howard County's only choice was suburban sprawl—or Columbia.

The would-be developers made the additional promise that Columbia would not be a burden on Howard County, either financially or aesthetically. The New Town would pay more in taxes than it would get back in services. Over twenty percent of the land, about 3,500 acres, would remain permanent open space, they continued, open to anyone who wanted to walk through the woods, around the lakes, or in the parks. Furthermore, Columbia would provide new and better shopping facilities, recreational areas, and cultural and entertainment opportunities for the whole county.

It was costing Rouse $5,000 a day in interest on the $23 million he owed, many people knew, so it was apparent that, for him, Columbia was not simply a way to make a quick buck. Perhaps, people began to feel, Rouse was something more than a typical developer.

Then along came what seemed a crushing blow—a brief by the County Attorney's office giving the opinion that rezoning for a New Town was probably illegal in the State of Maryland. Rouse was no longer the huge developer out to ruin Howard County, but the object of sympathy. People began to rally to his support. One woman organized a trip to Cherry Hill Shopping Center in southern New Jersey to show what good work Rouse did. At an important open meeting before the zoning board, not a single hostile citizen showed up.

Almost a year after Rouse announced his intention to build a New Town in Howard County, he went back to the county office with his plan. On an eight foot by eight foot map, colored areas showed high density, low density, and medium density residential areas, industry, open space, and how they all fit together. The three county commissioners found a way to get past the sticky legal matters mentioned in the attorney's brief, and voted into effect a special kind of New Town Zoning for developments of over 2,500 acres.

The second great hurdle had been cleared. And yet, in terms of creating a better living environment—"A Garden for People to Grow In," as Rouse phrased it—Columbia had just begun.


Columbia calls itself "the next America." Its planning, however, was as much a reaction against typical city building as it was a project for a new and better way. In a perceptive speech in 1966, James Rouse described exactly what Columbia was reacting against. "Let's look at how our cities grow. A farm is sold and begins raising houses instead of potatoes. Then another farm goes. Forests are cut. Valleys are filled. Streams are buried in storm sewers. Kids overflow the schools. A new school is built. Churches come out of the basement. Then more schools, more churches, traffic grows, roads are widened, front yards cut back to make room for the automobiles. Service stations are built; Tasty Freeze, MacDonald Hamburgers pockmark the old highway. Enough traffic now to make a good spot for a shopping center and a developer. Maybe we build it. Maybe you have a branch bank in it. Now the traffic is strangled. We need to build an expressway, so we hack through the landscape with a new freeway and this crosses the old road and creates a cloverleaf. And now there's a spot for a regional shopping center. We build it and surely you have a branch bank here. Then office buildings, and then with this concentration come high-rise apartments. Thus, the bits and pieces of cities are splattered across the landscape."

Columbia would be different. There, all the elements of a city would be brought together into a single, coherent whole. If Rouse did not know exactly what kind of city he wanted, he was excited by the possibilities and instilled this excitement into his whole organization. A church and an office building, he would point out, are rarely used at the same time. If they were placed next to each other, they could share a single parking lot and keep parts of the city from going dead after dark and on Sundays.

Rouse fully accepted the basic premises of the New Town idea. Only when it came to encircling the town in a greenbelt did he, like so many other private developers, break with Garden City and New Town principles. He simply could not afford the expense of a greenbelt, he explained, especially because he was committed to leaving so much internal land as permanent open space.

Rouse and his planners took an unusual step before settling down to create a plan for Columbia. They held a series of meetings with what they considered the "people" experts in our society. This did not mean turning over the landscaping to a minister and the road system to a doctor, but it meant getting their ideas on the best possible educational system, health system, and living environment generally, at least in abstract terms. Then the architects could, for example, plan around the idea of many small schools as opposed to a few large ones, knowing that this scheme had a high priority in the mind of the developer and his advisors.

The actual physical plan for Columbia introduced no revolutionary ideas, but there is a distinct slant to the way Columbia used basic New Town concepts. One of the fundamental questions the planners addressed themselves to was how to make Columbia urban and exciting without making it impersonal and alienating. They decided that building on a human scale was the first priority and, therefore, ruled out the erection of a fifteen story apartment building like Reston's Heron House. They tried, nevertheless, to create an urban atmosphere by focusing the diverse and varied activities of urban life in the village centers and the downtown area.

The next question was how to make Columbia a human city, in which people could feel like known individuals, at least in their own neighborhoods. Columbia went beyond any previous New Town in applying the neighborhood principle and in making each neighborhood separate and distinct.

The plan works this way: Each neighborhood consists of 800 to 1,200 families. At the center is an elementary school and a community center. Some have a small food store or snack bar and all have play areas and a swimming pool. The housing and pathway systems are then designed so that every child can walk safely and easily to school and every parent can do some shopping on foot.

Three neighborhoods make up a village. The villages, seven in all, are autonomous entities, each of which will hopefully develop the friendliness and cooperative spirit of a small town. To foster this small town feeling, the planners have separated the villages by walkways, fields, and woods.

The plans call for a Village Center that contains a supermarket, laundry, restaurants, and most of the other basic shops and services. Each center is to be different from the others in architecture and in the stores and facilities it offers. A typical one might include a large swimming pool, a skating rink, a teen center, and some distinctive building such as an old barn that has been converted into a theater and community center. Tennis courts, playing fields, tot lots, walkways, bikeways, a middle school, and a high school are also to be part of each village.

Downtown Columbia will consist of a combination of office buildings, landscaped pavilions, and a spectacular mall. The downtown area is being made particularly attractive by an artificial body of water, Lake Kittamaqundl. This is one of three man-made lakes to be created in Columbia, and is only possible, as Rouse explains, because Columbia is such a large project. He calculates that Columbia's first two lakes will cost over $1.5 million. A builder acquiring a few hundred, or even a few thousand, acres could not possibly absorb this kind of cost, but spread over 15,000 acres, as at Columbia, the lakes add only $100 per acre to the land cost.

The physical plan for Columbia, then, is essentially a refined version of the plans that have evolved from Letchworth and the British New Towns, through Radburn, Greenbelt, and Reston. Radburn's separation of pedestrian and automobile traffic, for example, is incorporated into the Columbia plan, with additional consideration given to bicycle and horseback riding.

Aerial view of Columbia.

The plans for Columbia strike out in a new direction in the development of community services. Rouse felt that a New Town had the opportunity to provide its inhabitants with something beyond a pleasant, functional environment. More than any New Town developer in the United States, he has attempted to organize social as well as physical services, and in this he has made a significant contribution to the basic theory behind New Town building. His efforts in this direction have also made Columbia into a testing ground for ideas that can be applied elsewhere.

Rouse persuaded the Johns Hopkins Medical School of Baltimore to join in the building of Columbia by setting up a city-wide health program that offers residents comprehensive health care, including doctors, hospital treatment, psychiatric help, ambulance service, and maternity care at relatively low costs. Since most of the expense for medical treatment is paid in a monthly fee, subscribers tend to use fully the services they have paid for. This means that people have regular physical check-ups and go to the doctors at the first sign of disease. The result has been a substantial decrease in hospitalization for people on the plan.

In the field of education, the emphasis in Columbia has been on small schools and on experimentation. The Howard County Board of Education obtained a Ford Foundation grant to try out open classrooms, team teaching, and other innovative techniques. Columbia also has established a network of child care centers and supervised play areas for six- to twelve-year-olds. Three universities have added to the cultural and educational opportunities in Columbia, particularly for adults.

In the area of communication, Rouse envisioned an elaborate

cable television system that would allow for community stations, educational programing, and a range of other services. Time-Life, Inc. agreed to build one of the most sophisticated systems anywhere, even complying with the prescription against over-head wires in Columbia. Unfortunately, the scheme fell apart when the county could not settle the matter of franchise rights.

The biggest disappointment in Columbia, and to Rouse person-ally, has come in the area of public transportation. He wanted Columbia to lead the way in cutting down the reliance on the car. He also wanted a system that would pay for itself. The planners designed into Columbia a system of roads for buses only, to be used by a fleet of minibuses that would circulate through the city continuously. The system was tried and the re-sult was that the minibuses were little used.

Now a system called Columbus has taken over. It attempts to achieve a compromise between the taxi and the bus, going to in-dividual homes like a taxi, but making numerous stops and charg-ing a low rate like a bus. So far the system has not enjoyed wide use, but gas shortages may change this situation.

Perhaps the most farsighted planning has come in the organiza-tion of Columbia's religious facilities. Instead of building ten or twenty churches and saddling each congregation with an enor-mous financial burden, Rouse encouraged the ministers, rabbis, and priests to build and share a common facility. This pooling of resources brings the additional advantage of closer cooperation between all the religious groups.

Finally, in organizing cultural events, Columbia's developers have made bold initiatives. These include building a 5,000 seat outdoor auditorium and contracting the Washington National

Symphony to play thirty concerts there each summer for the next twenty years.

In 1966, when Columbia was more a dream and a plan than a city, Rouse explained what he hoped were the larger implications of what he was doing. "Urban growth is our opportunity not our enemy" he declared. "It invites us to correct the past, to build new places that are productive for business and for the people who live there, places that are infused with nature and stimulating to man's sense of beauty, places that are in scale with people and so formed as to encourage and give strength to a real community which will enrich life, build character and personality, promote concern, fellowship, brotherhood." These might well be the words of Ebenezer Howard, spelled out so many decades ago!

As Route 29 enters Columbia, it abruptly becomes a landscaped parkway with no overhead wires, billboards, or hamburger stands. Walk or drive through Columbia and look for litter—there is almost none. The townhouses and garden apartments, too, with their crisp lines and fresh appearance, enhance the feeling of the sparkling newness of this town.

Of those who live in Columbia, young married people seem the best adjusted and most able to take advantage of the opportunities. B. Owen Williams, a young lawyer who bicycles to work each day at the American City Building in downtown Columbia, described Columbia as "absolutely ideal for a young family with young children."

A special innovation in Columbia is the large, temperature-regulated mall. Rouse realized from experience what Howard had foreseen in his plans, that a well-designed mall can become more than just a place to shop. It can be the focal point of a community. The mall at Columbia was designed with this idea in mind, and, already, it functions as a community center for a wide range of activities from picnic lunches to the annual Spring Ball.

The goals of Columbia, as defined by Rouse and his staff, are still highly idealistic. Columbia, they claim, will have a balance of income groups, large amounts of open space, beautiful land-scaping, and all the services and amenities to make it "the best possible environment for the growth of people." On the other hand, the Rouse company is not simply building a dream city, but fully expects to make a large financial profit. Are these two aims compatible?

Rouse thinks they are. Competing on the open market, he argues, is the best way to find out what people really want. Rouse took an enormous risk in building the town because he felt that people would be willing to pay highly for the end product. In this sense, Columbia represents what Rouse feels is American business at its best, business that "seeks to discover needs, finds ways of serving them, and receives rewards for its efforts."

How much money Columbia makes is important to Rouse not only because his company depends on profits for its survival and growth, but also because, if Columbia makes a substantial profit, Rouse feels other developers will copy its example. Unlike Rad-burn, which hoped to inspire imitators because it functioned so well and met an important housing need so sensibly, Columbia

Weatherproof shopping mall in Columbia.

hopes to inspire imitators with the additional incentive of big profits. This it seems likely to do.

For all of Rouse's arguments, however, it might have been better if Howard's limited profits approach had caught on. Future New Town developers may not be as daring or as socially sensitive as Rouse. In search of maximum profits, these developers might be tempted to cut corners and avoid bold, innovative experiments, in which case they may end up with glorified middle and upper class suburbs instead of New Towns.

But, fortunately, the Rouse Company has skill and social vision, and is in a class by itself in the way it has calculated and managed the economics of building a city from scratch. The company went further than any previous New Town venture in setting up economic models. The developers calculated that they would have to build and sell over 2,000 housing units per year and build a city of at least 100,000 people in order to be successful financially, given the cost and size of their site. Even so, they concluded, the expenses of land development, taxes, and interest would be greater than the profit from land sales and rent for the first six years. Only then would the project begin to make money.

To meet this demanding building schedule, Columbia has to capture a disproportionately large share of Maryland's housing market, year after year. But in a remarkable demonstration of salesmanship and business skills, the company has been able to stay close enough to its original schedule that after exactly seven years Columbia has begun to show a profit. This it should continue to do in greater and greater amounts until 1980, when the city will have its 110,000 inhabitants.

Probably the most encouraging point about Columbia (and New Towns that have followed its lead) is that its ideal of the good life is based on inclusion rather than exclusion. Black and white people live next to each other in Columbia, as do people with a variety of incomes. Residents consider this one of its advantages.

Although Rouse was deeply concerned with making Columbia profitable, he did feel it was important for the town to have an economic mix. To accomplish this goal, it was necessary to seek government subsidies for low-income housing. He was able to obtain some (though not all) of the aid he wanted. As a result, in the same neighborhood one finds both a $70,000 detached house and a group of government subsidized townhouses for families with low incomes. Central mailboxes at which one meets neighbors each day help to make for a friendly neighborhood. The attitude of wanting to get to know people who are not necessarily from one's own social, economic, or ethnic background is the reason Columbia is suceeding in welding its heterogeneous population into a community.

Most suburbs fear that industry will mar the landscape and pollute the air and water. Columbia's developers have sought out industry, feeling that it is irresponsible to build a beautiful environment by polluting someone elses, and they are trying to find ways to reduce pollution through new technology. At first, the planners calculated that they should provide 30,000 jobs, one per family. That figure has now been raised to 60,000. With the arrival of the General Electric plant, with its 12,000 jobs, Columbia should have no problem in meeting this goal. And Columbia promises that every person who works in the town will be able to afford to live there.

The ideal of inclusion rather than exclusion can also be seen in Columbia's attitude toward population density. By winning the fight for zoning in Howard County, Columbia will have more people on less land than most suburbs, but views this concentration of people as an important element in creating an exciting urban environment.

Columbia is not utopia and is troubled by many of the same problems facing the rest of our society. For example, two of the teen centers at one time became "black turf," indicative of racial tensions. Drug traffic, too, has always existed in Columbia and has even been heavy at times. Crime has also found its way in, burglary leading the list.

In spite of these problems, people in Columbia feel they are truly part of this New Town and hence part of something exciting and different. As one woman put it, "We can try here—try out new ideas and try to make it a better and better city."

In the next five or ten years, Rouse hopes to start two more New Towns, and Columbia's success has spurred new interest in New Town building. Recently General Electric announced it will begin building a New Town in southern New Jersey in connection with the Seabrook Farms industry. But the most encouraging result of all, stemming from Columbia, Reston, and New Towns begun in California and elsewhere, is that their example has spurred the United States Government to step once more into the general field of community development and the special field of helping to create New Towns.

# Chapter 8   Re-Enter the Federal Government

It was in the troubled mid-1960s that Reston and Columbia came into being. These new towns were conceived at a time when some of our country's domestic problems were particularly acute —widespread rioting and burning on city streets, a growing population with an ever-mounting need for decent places to live, the "keep-out" zoning restrictions in land-gobbling suburbs.

At this juncture, it seemed that New Towns might indeed offer a possible, if only partial, solution to the plight of the cities. Yet it was obvious from the start that despite valiant efforts, private developers could not afford to build complete new towns for people of all economic levels. If low-income housing were to be built, it had to be subsidized.

Might not the federal government be the logical and essential partner in building these new communities? This was the question President Lyndon Johnson asked, and it was he who became the real driving force behind the legislation that brought the United States Government back into the New Town movement.

In January, 1964, eleven months before the first people moved into Reston, Johnson surprised the Congress by initiating action in this field. He unexpectedly asked for federal funds to assist local governments in acquiring land and comprehensively planning for the orderly development of new communities.

Congress was taken by surprise, and it sent the request to committee, where it was pigeonholed. But Johnson was not a man to give up easily.

On March 2, 1965, he sent a message to Congress entitled "Problems and Future of the Central City and Its Suburbs." These were the dimensions of the problems of the city as he saw them:

> At the end of the century—in less than 40 years—urban population will double, and we will have to build in our cities as much as we have built since the first colonists arrived on these shores. It is as if we had 40 years to rebuild the entire urban United States.

New Towns, of course would be only a small part of this rebuilding; but they could be a useful tool especially in areas of rapid urban growth.

Despite the President's plea, Congress still hesitated. Then, in 1968, the Johnson administration made the final thrust to get the needed legislation passed. This time the push was successful. In his waning months in office, the President signed the necessary bill into law and, for the first time since the era of the Greenbelt Towns, the federal government became involved in supporting the building of New Towns.

The Housing and Urban Development Act of 1968 (amended and revised in 1970) spelled out precisely how the new partnership of government and private enterprise was to work. Developers were to submit a master plan to the Department of Housing and Urban Development (HUD), outlining exactly what kind of town they wished to build, the range and mix of income groups the town would accommodate, and the kinds of innovations and experiments that would be tried. A certain number of New Towns, which fit the bill's elaborate requirements, would then be chosen for federal assistance. The government's end of the bargain was to finance, through loan guarantees, the land purchase and the installation of certain necessary facilities such as water mains and sewers.

Before a developer or development corporation could qualify for this assistance, it was necessary to convince HUD that the town to be built was a genuine town and not simply a suburban subdivision; that the new community could offer a substantial number of jobs; and that it would contribute to the social and economic welfare of the surrounding area.

Furthermore, the New Town must be designed to increase the available choices for living and working for the fullest possible range of people of different incomes and ethnic groups. Developer, contractors, and industries all had to give assurance of "affirmative efforts" to encourage and help people from minority groups to make their homes in the new community. The aim was to make certain that each selected New Town be truly an open, "equal opportunity" town.

By 1974, sixteen new communities in ten states had been chosen by HUD to receive federal aid under the New Communities legislation. These sixteen communities were to cover approximately

90,000 acres of land, and house, when completed, over 900,000 people.

Each of the proposed communities is unique. Maumelle, Arkansas, plans to have an experimental system of educational parks, instead of traditional schools. Flower Mound, Texas, between Dallas and Fort Worth, is a new town developing construction methods to combat noise pollution from the nearby airport. Riverton and Ganada, both near Rochester, New York, are planning new, innovative social services. And Soul City, in rural North Carolina, is the first "free-standing" (as opposed to satellite) New Town to receive a commitment of federal assistance, and the first in which the principal sponsor is a black-owned enterprise.

Rather than discuss all the new communities, this chapter will concentrate on two—both in Minnesota. Jonathan was the first of the federally funded new communities to secure the coveted HUD guarantee, a twenty-one million dollar sum for the first ten years of development.

The story of Jonathan began in the fall of 1965. At that time, 5,000 acres of land were assembled twenty miles southwest of Minneapolis in an area of rapid growth. The property was later enlarged to 8,000 acres. One of the unusual things about this New Town site is that it lies within the borders of the small town of Chaska, population 4,000. In five years, the population of Jonathan is expected to equal that of Chaska and, if all goes according to plan, in twenty years Jonathan should have 50,000 residents. This would make the Jonathan—Chaska complex a city of perhaps 60,000.

As of 1974, the people of Jonathan participate in the municipal processes of their parent city. As citizens of Chaska, they receive a number of municipal services, such as electric power, sewer plant facilities, and fire and police protection. As residents of Carver County, they also have a voice in decisions regarding county services. On the community level, through the Jonathan Association, residents can become involved in the planning and running of the town's local activities.

Jonathan is easily accessible to Minneapolis and other areas through a series of interconnected highways. The main line of the Chicago–Milwaukee railroad passes through the town, a feature especially important to industry. As Jonathan grows, the hope is that it will be a prime candidate for a local and regional mass transit system.

The 50,000 prospective residents of Jonathan are to be housed in five villages similar to those in Reston and Columbia. There are to be several industrial parks, and a continuous network of open space and wooded areas. A protecting greenbelt will be made up of a state-owned Arboretum and University Fruit Farm, a deep ravine system, a lake road, and a game farm.

The development of Jonathan, over a twenty year span, should have a flexibility of design that will allow the community to change and adapt as future needs require and new technologies permit.

The plans for Jonathan contain the major elements suggested by Ebenezer Howard—a limited size, a greenbelt, an inner network of open space, a flexibility of design. For its residents, it provides for a full life, including both work and play. The outstanding difference between Ebenezer Howard's plan and Jonathan's is the latter's physical and political tie with another city.

In appearance, Jonathan resembles other New Towns, with flower beds along the entrance, attractive wooden signs pointing the way to the Information Center and the Jonathan Art Center, clusters of brand-new single family and row houses, and the colorful village square.


Jonathan's origin and its present direction owe a debt to Henry McKnight, who died in February, 1973. Everyone on the staff at Jonathan seemed to know him personally and to have "McKnight stories" to tell.

According to one man, "McKnight believed heart and soul in the New Town idea and he knew just what was necessary to make that dream of his come true. First, he had to convince the local bankers and businessmen to join him. What he did was to invite them out to his place in the country. They came in their business suits, all slicked up. The first thing you know, they were piled onto a hay wagon and driven to a picnic area for a barbecue. Coats came off, sleeves were rolled up, and everyone relaxed. In this mellow atmosphere, Henry won the day for his cause."

McKnight had an important attribute that made him different from most developers and that proved invaluable to Jonathan. He was a politician. He served in the Minnesota State Senate and he also knew his way around Washington. He knew the people to contact and how to get things moving.

McKnight was not above using some rather unconventional

tactics when he was not getting his way. One undersecretary of HUD, for example, found the Minnesotan, armed with two cups of coffee, encamped in front of the door of his office when he arrived at eight in the morning. There was no possible ducking out for the HUD official.

McKnight could pull off this kind of stunt without antagonizing people. "You couldn't help liking him," an officer of the Jonathan Development Corporation remarked. "He inspired confidence; people respected and trusted him." And so he was able to move the mountains of Washington's bureaucracy. It was largely because of the confidence this man inspired that Jonathan obtained HUD's first bond guarantee.

McKnight was also an avid conservationist. He was such a nature enthusiast that he insisted a road and water pipes be made to bend around a big old tree he thought should be saved. That "Friendship Tree" is one of Jonathan's prized landmarks.

Walking around Jonathan, one notices that conservation guidelines have been used to preserve as much of nature's ecological balance as possible. All trees are left standing on steep slopes, and there is minimal disturbance of ground cover on gentler slopes. The continuous network of open space and tree-filled areas gives human beings and wildlife a reasonable chance to share common territory. Restricted use of ecologically harmful chemical fertilizers, pesticides, and herbicides add to the likelihood of this peaceful coexistence continuing.

Good air quality is maintained in Jonathan. Ear and eye pollution are minimized by vegetation and earthwork barriers that shield bothersome but necessary activities, such as auto traffic.

As for industry, Jonathan put its very earliest efforts into attracting a large variety of firms, and has been remarkably successful in developing its industrial parks. Early on, a Swedish toothpaste manufacturing concern decided to open an American plant at Jonathan. Though the company had at first chosen another location in Minnesota, the owner, already oriented to the many advantages of Sweden's planned communities, decided that his plant belonged in the rising New Town.

Though Jonathan has not gone in for heavy industry, there are already more than two dozen varieties of the light kind—medical research and products, hydraulic equipment, canning, cosmetics, electronics, computers, water purification systems. Recently, some townhouses have been added to Jonathan's industrial complex. These are for sale or rent to very small companies, who need little more than office space.

By starting the town of Jonathan with a firmly established industrial base, the theory was this: A number of industries, offering a wide range of job opportunities, would act as a magnet, attracting a large variety of people. When the first industrial park was nearing completion, housing too was well under way. It was expected that people—all kinds of people—would be quick to follow.

Jonathan seems to have been rather more successful in attracting industry than in finding homeowners. This is a switch from the history of Radburn and the Greenbelt Towns.

The great variety in housing design in Jonathan is quite impressive. Six private developers, as well as the Jonathan Housing Corporation itself, were responsible for this. Private builders are

Jonathan's Treeloft apartments.

encouraged to take part in the development of Jonathan, but their plans must be reviewed and approved by the corporation, to ensure that there is conformity with the overall plan. A future resident may buy a ready-made house or may purchase land and select his own architect-builder, whose plans must also be officially approved. Townhouses and apartments are constructed for those who wish to rent rather than purchase their living quarters.

A particularly imaginative design characterizes the Treeloft apartments. They are built of modular units—complete, industrially manufactured sections—which are stacked much as a child's building blocks might be put together. The Treeloft apartments were built by the Jonathan Corporation at low rentals, for singles or very small families.

There are also higher priced, expandable, modular houses for growing families, developed by Standard Research Institute of California and built by the corporation. New modules or completed units can be added to these houses, to fulfill the need for added space.

Aesthetically attractive "inner space" patio homes, erected by a private California builder, feature a unique design in which the indoor living areas are oriented around a private garden court. One of the model homes features an electronically operated retractable roof—a useful innovation that makes the court livable during at least part of Minnesota's long winter season.

A negative aspect of Jonathan is that all similarly priced and styled houses are grouped together. The Jonathan Corporation is defensive about this practice. One of its officers explained that economic considerations dictate building in this fashion. It is just too expensive, he declared, for the various developers to scatter their buildings far and wide. There is, he says, no alternative but to build in block units. One wonders if there is really no way to solve this problem.

To counteract this segregation by income, the Jonathan Corporation makes all kinds of efforts to break down social barriers. High visibility makes it impossible to avoid seeing one's neighbors. Common walkways are hopefully conducive to more than nodding acquaintance. Group mailboxes are strategically located, to provide opportunities for people to meet each other and talk. Shared open spaces are designed to stimulate mixing among various groups. In addition, everyone living in Jonathan is automatically a member of the Jonathan Association, with its numerous activities and responsibilities.

There are a number of imaginative play structures linked to the housing areas. It is not uncommon for children in one neighborhood to shout "Let's go over to the Pirate Ship today," and interaction between the youngsters of the two areas then takes place spontaneously.

Jonathan has several lakes, and the Lake Grace Pavilion and Beach is a facility open to all residents. A particularly impressive feature is the waterfront around the lake, left free of development and reserved as a "pleasuring ground" for the whole community. Unlike Reston, Jonathan has decided to forego the financial advantage of high priced housing on this lake-front property.

One of Jonathan's most innovative programs is interactive cable TV. "Interactive" means a two-way cable television hook-up,

Pirate Ship playground in Jonathan.

linking individual subscribers with almost any kind of facility or service. Perhaps the best way to visualize the system is an illustration: A high school class, equipped with the necessary apparatus, is connected, through the Center, with a druggist at the local pharmacy. The students see the druggist go about his everyday business. They look over his shoulder, so to speak, while he prepares prescriptions and fills orders. A monitor, placed on the drug counter, enables the druggist to keep an eye on the class. He explains what he is doing, talks about his career, and answers questions from curious students.

This program is one of a series whose purpose is to give students a perspective on what goes on in the working world, and to assist them in making tentative career decisions. The program is also part of a demonstration project designed to show the possible applications of two-way TV.

There are many, many other possible applications, such as new health care services, in which, for example, a physician too busy in his hospital to pay outside calls can communicate visually with a home patient, as if he or she were in the doctor's office. In fact, with the help of a medical technician, the doctor could give a patient a complete medical examination and make a tentative diagnosis, because cable TV can focus so closely that an observer can read on his screen the date printed on a dime.

Information on traffic and travel, a burglar alarm security system, interactive games, data processing, fire protection, and library information are but a few of the other possibilities.

But which, from among a myriad of services, do people really want, and want sufficiently to become paying subscribers? Funding from HUD has enabled a group to do research on this question.

A New Town is, of course, an ideal place to conduct such an experiment. Cables can be laid without the extensive and expensive ripping up that would be necessary in an older city. Furthermore, the residents of a New Town are quite apt to be oriented toward innovation. The outcome of the experiment at Jonathan should provide needed guidelines in the development of this revolutionary and exciting two-way communications tool.

Still another new tool is Jonathan's Simulation Model, which enables planners to take a step-by-step look at their development decisions. By means of this computerized model, the planners are able to examine the impact of possible decisions—how many and what kinds of factories to permit, for example—twenty years into the future. Changes may be made at any point if the projected impact—on job opportunities, water supply, air quality, traffic flow—indicates an unwise course of action. Thus Jonathan is monitored to make corrections and changes as it goes along. It can be unusually sensitive to future needs, and always alert to the potential of new technology. Jonathan hopes to be a city that continually renews itself.

Jonathan also hopes to share with others some of its facilities and abilities. For this purpose, it has been paired with a "New Town-in-Town," Cedar-Riverside, in the heart of Minneapolis.

A New Town-in-Town differs from an outlying New Town in the smaller amount of land it occupies, the higher density of its population, and the absence of industrial parks. In a sense, a

New Town aims to be a small city. A New Town-in-Town aims to be a unique but integral part of a large city.

Jonathan and Cedar-Riverside differ widely. Jonathan, with its 8,000 acres of open countryside, will eventually be the home of some 50,000 people. Cedar-Riverside, on a mere 340 acres of city-scape, is planned to house about 30,000 with a projected daily influx of 30,000 workers, shoppers, students, and theater-goers.

Though twenty-five miles distant from one another, Jonathan and Cedar-Riverside have been paired since infancy. Pairing, in the case of communities, implies an interchange, by means of which one town directly benefits the other. This involves exchange of new ideas, sharing of experts, and exchanges of cultural and recreational facilities. Eventually, pairing might also foster housing swaps among residents as their needs and life styles change. Since both Jonathan and Cedar-Riverside are in the early stages of development, pairing so far has consisted mainly in sharing ideas, advisors, and a board member.

Although Cedar-Riverside is not a New Town in the strict definition of the term, HUD has included it in its New Communities operations. It was the first New Town-in-Town to receive HUD's coveted aid—a 24 million dollar loan guarantee. After this occurred, in 1971, massive concrete structures began to pierce the Minneapolis skyline.

The site of Cedar-Riverside is on the west bank of the Mississippi River, only twelve blocks from the downtown area of Minneapolis. Until the 1930s, this section contained a stable but poor Scandinavian community, inhabited by lumberjacks and river workers. As this kind of work grew scarce during the Depression,

Cedar-Riverside—the plan.

people moved out and the neighborhood deteriorated. By 1960 the population had fallen from 20,000 to 4,000 people.

The Cedar-Riverside New Town-in-Town story, then, begins in the early 1960s with a decayed, run-down city area. Here, many of the two story frame houses stood sagging and empty. The shops and stores, except for a few shabby bars, beer joints, and a 1930-style burlesque show, were mostly boarded up. The only reminders of better days were an old private college and two hospitals on the fringes of the decayed residential section.

Regardless of decay, this section was well-located, close to the heart of Minneapolis and just across the river from the main campus of the University of Minnesota. This institution badly needed space, so it decided to locate its West Campus on the borders of the old Swedish neighborhood. Blueprints were ready by 1960.

In 1963, a new public housing project for the elderly was erected in the old residential area. Things were beginning to happen in a section of the city that had seemed destined for the ash heap.

And then, the essential happened—the right person, the right place, and the right time converged. The right person was Mrs. Gloria Segal, an energetic and magnetic woman steeped in the educational, cultural, and civic activities of Minneapolis. She and her husband and their friend, Keith Heller, an official of the University of Minnesota, decided that erecting a small walk-up apartment house in this old section of town would be a good investment. Having acquired suitable property, they engaged the services of Ralph Rapson, head of the University's School of Architecture, to help them with their project.

Professor Rapson persuaded the trio to raise their sights and to consider the revival of the entire area in which their small apartment house was to stand. The idea caught on and before long the Segal-Heller group acquired more and more property and was able to interest others in doing the same.

In addition, Mrs. Segal and her group stimulated the planning and renewal officials of Minneapolis to study the area and to issue a report. Action followed quickly. By 1968 a renewal plan had been drawn up for the entire Cedar-Riverside section.

Eventually, the various private groups that had acquired property merged, forming a development organization known as Cedar-Riverside Associates. Then Henry McKnight joined as an investor and backer. McKnight brought with him the wealth of experience he had gained as a prime force behind the Jonathan project.

The rebuilding of Cedar-Riverside as a New Town demonstrates the unique cooperation that can take place among such widely different groups as a private association, a municipal government, and a state university. Furthermore, the project represents a significant advance in the art of planning.

The redevelopment part of the project calls for five neighborhoods of 6,000 people each, to be built over a period of twenty years. One neighborhood is already well under way.

Unlike most other New Towns, Cedar-Riverside has been able to offer a chance for mixing in a new way. Cedar-Riverside's tall apartment houses are designed for the rich and the poor and those in between. People of all races and economic levels are housed in the same buildings, in similar apartments. There is

Cedar-Riverside—the reality.

nothing to show which family pays the maximum of $550 a month, and which the minimum of $50. In the latter instance, the balance of the rent is paid through federal subsidies.

The plaza, with its balconied high-rise apartments on one side and its new four story row houses on the other, is an attractive complex. One does not have the sense of being hemmed in, a feeling one experiences in the canyons of brick and steel in so many large cities. Rather, there is an atmosphere of openness and airiness, accentuated by the fact that there is not a single car in the entire area. Automobiles are garaged in four parking levels below ground. The plazas, parks, and playgrounds will all be linked together by walkways and bicycle trails in a safe and attractive pattern.

An imaginatively designed "Centrum" will be the focal point for large shops and offices, indoor sports, social service agencies, religious services, movies, and the performing arts. Each neighborhood will have its own shops, open spaces, and child care and health service facilities. In all these ways this New Town-in-Town will resemble its older models. Cedar-Riverside differs from typical New Towns in some obvious ways: The institutional jobs are already there and more and more commercial jobs are being added, so that industrial parks are unnecessary. Central city work is within walking distance and other employment is an easy commute on major highways. Cedar-Riverside rises vertically because it cannot spread horizontally, and offers a modified kind of Garden City living in the midst of a large metropolis.

Because of its plan for high density development, this new type of New Town is an ideal laboratory for testing possible solutions to some of our most vexing inner city problems. Many of these problems relate to people living in close proximity to, yet feeling isolated and alienated from, one another.

"Cedar-Riverside will be people oriented," according to its director of planning and development. "People will be the focal point for planning and people will provide the vitality and variety that make the cosmopolitan setting so interesting and vibrant." He adds this note: "In the urban New Town, the cityscape will replace the landscape, offering its own beauty and appeal."

Today's urgent need for both the birth of new cities in land-scapes and the rebirth of old ones in cityscapes may well profit by stretching the definition of a New Town. Both Jonathan and Cedar-Riverside are relying on principles laid down by Ebenezer Howard; both are innovative by their very nature. Because of this experimental quality, Jonathan and Cedar-Riverside, as well as other New Towns, are trying out new technological inventions —systems for moving people and handling goods, new approaches to heating, refuse disposal, and communications. Where, better than in a New Town, can the newer technologies be tested in a living environment?

Chapter **9** New Technologies and New Towns

Imagine a city floating like a water lily. A pipe dream? The idea grew out of the discovery of something called a Flip Ship, a specially designed hollow cylinder that stands upright in the water and supports an enormous weight on its head. The head projects out of the water and remains steady in even the roughest water.

Three Flip Ships could support a platform as big as a city block, with office buildings and apartment houses on top. Link enough platforms together and it would be possible to plan and build a New Town that is a floating city. The town would have a number of advantages, but the biggest is that it could be floated a couple of miles outside any harbor in the world. It's possible that it could be towed from one site to another.

Is this one form New Towns of the future will take? The technology clearly exists to build such cities. In fact, if United States engineer John Craven and Japanese architect Kiyonori Kikutake have their way, they will show just how feasible it is to build floating cities, by constructing a floating platform of twenty square blocks off the coast of Waikiki, and making it the site of Hawaii's bicentennial exhibition in 1976.

Flip Ships are perhaps the most radical way in which new technology may alter the shape of New Towns in the coming years. But technological innovations will also alter the shape and functioning of the New Towns to be built on dry land in the next decade or two.

New Towns are ideal laboratories for testing out the new ideas made possible by new technologies. The two-way cable setup in Jonathan; Columbia's system of minibuses; and a pneumatic garbage collection system at Roosevelt Island, the New Town-in-Town just off Manhattan Island, are three examples. But what about the future? What kind of advanced technology will find its way into the next generation of New Towns?

New housing technology is among the most difficult to implement because, in making the large investment in buying a house, people tend to be conservative. They want to make sure they won't end up with a house they cannot sell. Considerable research has thus been devoted not so much to building new kinds of shelters, but to providing cheaper conventional-looking houses. This end seems best accomplished by mass producing houses in a factory and by creating new finishing materials such as spray-on plastics.

The technology is available today to build houses with movable walls so that as family needs change, room sizes and arrangements can be varied. Even stranger is the idea of building inflatable structures. The inflatables can be altered in size or shape with little difficulty. Furthermore, they have a translucent quality that seems to give a greater sense of space than areas enclosed by traditional solid walls.

Habitat is an imaginative alternative to conventional buildings.

Habitat's mass produced modules.

This unusual-looking structure was introduced at the 1967 Montreal Exposition in Canada. The handsome, individual prefabricated living units are attached to a zigzagging concrete structure that can be adjusted to fit the site. Each unit has its own outdoor terrace on the roof of another dwelling. Habitat appears to honor people's individuality in ways that impersonal, monotonous highrise apartments do not.

Another interesting possibility is for people to live in a domed city, an idea that has long been discussed but never tried. Our present technology makes possible the building of a weather-regulated geodesic dome over a good part or all of a town. Rather than cover an already existing city, a New Town offers the chance to design not only the dome but also the area inside, taking advantage of the fact that the enclosed buildings would not have to be constructed to withstand wind and weather. But would people really like living under a dome?

Technological advances have also been made in treatment of waste. The garbage truck is noisy and inefficient, and the town dump spoils land that could be used in better ways. Furthermore, the garbage itself can be a valuable resource and not simply something that pollutes our air, water, and land.

Garbage can be collected, for example, through a vacuum system of underground pipes, thus avoiding the problems that occur when refuse is placed on the streets. One such system (Automated Vacuum Collection—AVAC), has been tested since 1961 and is already in operation in Sweden and in Disney World in Florida. A similar system is being installed on New York City's Roosevelt Island. Refuse is deposited into the system and sucked through large steel pipes to a central collection point. The system works efficiently, with few breakdowns, and has proved economically sound for a high-density area of less than six square miles.

An even more exciting idea now being studied and tested by the Combustion Power Company of Palo Alto, California, is to pipe solid waste directly to a special incinerator that burns it under high temperature and pressure. The hot gases given off as the garbage burns are used to spin a turbine, which in turn drives an electric generator that might produce something like ten percent of the city's power.

Economical recycling is the ultimate goal of any garbage or sewage system. In ancient days, when organic wastes were returned directly to the land, the bigger the city, the richer the fields around it. Today we are trying to get back to this kind of recycling by converting garbage into a peat-like organic fertilizer and soil conditioner, but the high cost of separating out metal and glass has made it uneconomical in the past.

In recycling water, however, research is now far enough advanced so that it is predicted that by 1976 many commercial buildings will use systems to purify and recycle their own water. It is thought that these systems will also be used in most homes by the 1980s.

In the field of public transportation, Disney World in Florida has demonstrated the effectiveness of a monorail system in quickly moving large numbers of people from the parking lot to points throughout the park. Other similar transportation ideas, such as an Alden Capsule running on its own automated guideway and a

Sky Highway—the monorail at Disney World.

monocab system of suspended cars, are also workable. These systems will have difficulty, in present-day society, in competing with the privacy and convenience of a car, but if and when gas shortages force a reduced use of cars in town, any of these schemes might be substituted. A developer of a New Town might design a town around one of these systems and save space and money by building the town without roads.

Another possibility is that the next breakthrough in transportation systems will be in air travel. An airbus service, utilizing forty to eighty passenger short-take-off-and-landing planes, could easily become competitive with regular bus service for all but very short trips. Launching and landing pads—STOLports, they are called—take up comparatively little space. The biggest stumbling block right now is the volume of noise these sky coaches make.

This airbus system may be outmoded before it is implemented, however, by a transportation idea that may well reshape our society and our future. Bell Aerosystem's flying belt and Williams Research Corporation's personal flying platform, according to an MIT study, are operational, and the researchers predict general acceptance by the middle to late 1980s. Whether it means getting onto a small airborne raft or strapping on a motor, flying will give us a new freedom in choosing how we live and where we live. Problems of pollution and safety, of course, need to be considered and mastered before such vehicles are allowed to fill the skies.

Advances in new communications systems take us into the realm of science fiction, but the technology exists today and its products may well be upon us in the next ten to twenty years. The potential for changing the shape of our lives is fantastic. New

Communities may be the best places to try out the new freedoms technology will give us.

A two-way wireless TV would make audio-visual communication possible between individual people, and between a person and a film printer, a xerox machine, or an audio-visual recorder. The International Telephone and Telegraph Company (ITT) is working on this project and claims it has completed the basic technology. These computerized, battery-powered, hand-held, touch-tone videophones should have a world-wide hookup in the 1980s, according to reports from ITT.

As for computers, we have only begun to tap them for private use. Just as intriguing are video cassettes and facsimile reproduction machines, which can instantly print out audio messages, newspapers, magazines, and other verbal or printed material. This technology means that each home could become an information and communications center. These scientific advances could radically change the way people shop, do business, are educated, and get medical treatments. One could live anywhere, with distances from major facilities no longer important. New Communities could then be located with prime consideration given to access to recreation, agreeable climate, and natural beauty.

However, the shortages of energy and other resources may seriously affect the innovative plans of today's scientists and technicians. Institutions and scientists may have to reshuffle their priorities. Money and brain power might well be redirected, for example, into channels that will bring the widespread use of solar energy into being. Once again, New Towns are excellent testing grounds for putting theory into practice.

In thinking back over the many exciting possibilities that science and technology can offer us in New Towns and elsewhere, there are central questions to be asked. What kind of environment will be created? Can the wonders of technology be employed without people becoming machine-oriented robots?

For a preview of the future, step inside an imaginary dome and assume that a woman decides to tell about her life and how it is different from the way it used to be. This is what she might say:

I can't believe how much time I wasted driving in a car to shop, to market, and to take my older children hither and yon. Now, my youngsters can hike or bike anywhere in town. And shopping, cooking and other household chores take only an hour a day. I hold down a twenty-five-hour-a-week job and still have plenty of free time.

Where my computer hookup and picturephone come in so handy is when I need information. Last weekend, for example, our vacuum cleaner broke. So I hooked into a program that enabled my son and me to diagnose what was wrong. The necessary parts were conveyed through the large pneumatic tube that connects us with a supply depot. Then we plugged into a simple program that we followed step by step. We repaired the appliance ourselves without difficulty.

"Are there any features you don't like about living in this New Town?" one might query.

Yes, there are: I get frightened. Only last month there was a power failure. Everything—but literally *everything*—stopped. And I suddenly realized how utterly dependent we've become on a completely mechanized world in this New Town of ours. I didn't like the sensation I experienced—no, not a bit.

"How about your son? How does he feel?"

Oh, he's never known anything different, for he was a baby when we came here, and he looks at me strangely when I talk of the "good old days." He enjoys his school, which is highly individualized, using the whole community, indoors and outdoors, for teaching and learning. Yes, he likes that.

But, somehow, my boy reminds me of my own kid brother, who used to say, "Ma, there's nothing to do here." And a far-away look would come into his eyes. As a young man, he left home in search of a more adventurous life.

There's a lot more for kids to do in this New Town—all kinds of activities and clubs. But, once in a while, I see that same restless look in the eyes of my son, as he says to me, "Ma, there's nothing to do here." And I suspect that he, too, will set out, one fine day, in search of something new.

This imaginary excursion into the future is a reminder that people are people, no matter where or how they live. New Towns, with their planning and their applied technologies, can cut down on the time spent on dull, everyday chores. New Towns can be highly desirable places to live in light of our still unsolved energy crisis. While these New Communities are laboratories for resource-consuming advances in applied science, paradoxically they also make possible an old-fashioned and far less energy-consuming way of living. In a New Town, people can once more depend on their legs for locomotion. They can walk to work, to school, to shop, to visit. They can enjoy open country and greenery without traveling miles to do so. They can, by choice as well as necessity, lead a simplified life with far less discomfort than their counterparts in crowded cities or in isolated rural areas.

With their mixed economic and social base, with their expanded opportunities for work and play, and with their beautiful surroundings, New Communities can provide the means for a good life. There is small doubt of that. But can New Towns in and of themselves guarantee a full and satisfying life? That goal rests, as it always has, with people.

# Chapter 10 What About the Future?

New Towns in America are here to stay. Several are well on the path to becoming whole towns; others are completing their first or second village units. Some are in the process of breaking ground, while many others are waiting for HUD to act on their proposals. There are also dozens of additional New Town plans still on the drawing boards, waiting to be evaluated.

How do New Towns fit into the total pattern of the growing, mobile, and shifting population in our increasingly urbanized society? Though the rate of our population growth has recently shown a considerable and welcome drop, the post World War II baby boom is causing the formation of 27,000 new households every week. Although this may be a temporary phenomenon, it will add upward of 50 million people to our country in the next twenty-five years. Almost all of these people will settle in and around our largest cities. This means that our urban dilemmas will grow, not diminish, as we reach the end of the twentieth century.

The easiest solution to the increase in population is what we are all too adept at doing—allowing unplanned urban sprawl to spread its blight over some one million acres of land each year. The net result would be the ever deepening ills of overcrowding: inconvenience, traffic congestion, lack of open space, social stratification, and racial segregation.

There are, however, three other approaches available, no one of which can solve the problem alone. Taken together, they might well set us on a constructive, life-enriching path rather than an ecologically and socially disastrous one.

First, and perhaps most important because of the numbers of people involved, is the rescuing of large urban centers from decay and destruction. In most cities, this rescue operation is under way, but is progressing so slowly that ground is lost each year, as buildings get older and more middle class people flee to the suburbs. Continuing shortages of energy, however, may well cause a reversal of this trend.

Second is the strengthening of our smaller communities in both urban and rural regions, thereby transforming them into vital centers of life and activity. There has been an increasing concentration of interdependent activities in our society, centered mainly in metropolitan areas. Work opportunities of almost all varieties are therefore most abundant in the big cities and the nearby suburbs. Jobs in rural and small town America dry up. Young people often pull up roots and move to the big cities. But if some of these small towns can be reinvigorated with new industry and jobs, they can grow to a reasonable size and provide an alternative for those who do not want to leave or for others who would like to come.

These small towns need to grow if they are to become vital centers with plentiful work opportunities. The expansion of these communities, however, does not have to be chaotic. Advantage might well be taken of the same planning ideas and techniques that go into the creation of New Towns. Although the developer would have less flexibility than in building a New Town, the small town would already have roots in the past, and the expanded community could be a thoughtful mixing of old and new.

Often a prospering town—usually a suburb—is full of homes and estates for the well-to-do and has campus-like industries to help pay taxes and provide jobs. But it may lack housing for the lower paid people who work there. A town in this situation could become a New Community in spirit if this housing were supplied.

Finally, there is the option of starting from scratch and building New Towns from the ground up. This third alternative is creative, exciting, and practicable. New Towns can play an important role in America's urban growth and development.

Imaginative planners and developers are available to do the job, but developers can only go ahead when there is adequate financing. In recent years financial assistance has come from the private sector. Chase Manhattan Bank and the Connecticut Life Insurance Company, for example, actively participated in the construction financing of Columbia. A number of local banks have lent money to New Towns in their own areas.

The United States Government has gotten into the act through the Housing and Urban Development legislation of 1968 and 1970. State governments have also participated in efforts to bring about planned urban growth. New York was the first state to do so, through the creation of an Urban Development Corporation in 1968. UDC is aiding the construction of two New Towns in the state—Lysander, near Syracuse, and Audubon, close to Buffalo. The state agency is also helping to create a New-Town-in-Town—Roosevelt Island, on the East River just opposite Manhattan.

Regional governments and municipalities have also become active in the promotion of New Communities, both in and out of town. Thus all levels of government are now involved, at least to a small degree, in the New Town movement.

Yet, the available funding for New Communities is far below what is needed to get the job done. This is especially evident if one considers the goal set by the National Committee on Urban Growth—the immediate creation of one hundred New Communities the size of Columbia, in addition to ten new cities of at least one million people each.

David Rockefeller, Chairman of the Board of the Chase Manhattan Bank, has a suggestion for resolving the financial dilemma in the creation of New Towns. He proposes the formation of an agency, private or semi-public—perhaps a new kind of bank—to provide predevelopment financing. The new bank would seek its capital from commercial banks, insurance companies, industry, and other sources. Mr. Rockefeller even goes so far as to set a figure—ten billion dollars—as the capital this New Communities bank would need.

Mr. Rockefeller also suggests additional legislation to provide a suitable government agency with a better mechanism for acquiring land, so that sufficiently large and contiguous tracts can be purchased.

Following the British example, some government agency should, it seems, have the power to decide that it is in the public interest that certain land be used to build a New Community. The people who own that land should receive fair compensation, but their good fortune in owning land in a particular place should not entitle them to blackmailing the developer into paying an unreasonably high price, and thus forcing certain New Town projects to be abandoned.

One might think of New Towns as single links in the chain of organized growth. They can certainly never be a cure-all for urban ills. Planned urban growth cannot be fragmented; New Towns are only part of a much larger whole.

Nor are New Towns the answer for all people. They are at best one alternative. New Towns offer an unusual opportunity for those to whom the concept of blending the city and country into a harmonious entity has a particular appeal.

The New Town idea, from its original inception and as it has evolved through the years, is much more than an attractive Garden City. The New Town tells us something about our aspirations. New Towns are fresh starts. They are open communities freely available to people of all races, religions, and national origins. Furthermore, they make it possible for all residents, no matter what their economic level, to find suitable and decent housing in pleasant surroundings and to find the largest possible variety of work opportunities. In New Towns, all the parts fit together—housing, industry, shopping, open space, recreation, education—in an attempt to create a more perfect living environment for every human being.

But, after such a living environment has been created, the

proof of its success will depend on what the people who live there make of it. What they make of it depends on the good will, the energy, and the skill they bring to the task of keeping their New Town forever responsive to changing times and changing needs, forever new in spirit.

## Selected Reading List

Canty, Donald, ed.: *The New City*. National Committee on Urban Growth Policy. New York: Praeger; 1969.

Clapp, James A.: *New Towns and Urban Policy*. New York: Dunellen Pub. Co.; 1971.

Eichler, Edward P. and Kaplan, Marshall: *The Community Builders*. Berkeley and L.A.: U of California Press; 1967.

Howard, Ebenezer: *Garden Cities of Tomorrow*. ed. by Frederic J. Osborn. Cambridge, Mass.: MIT Press; 1965.

Jacobs, Jane: *The Death and Life of Great American Cities*. New York: Random House; 1961.

Mayer, Albert: *The Urgent Future: People, Housing, City, Region*. New York: McGraw Hill; 1967.

McHarg, Ian: *Design with Nature*. New York: Natural History Press; 1971.

Miller, Brown, Pinney, Neil and Saslow, William: *Innovation in New Communities*. Cambridge, Mass.: MIT Press; 1972.

Moynihan, Daniel P., ed.: *Toward a National Urban Policy*. New York: Basic Books; 1970.

145

Mumford, Lewis: *The Urban Prospect,* 1969; *Culture of Cities,* 1970; New York: Harcourt Brace Jovanovich.

Munzer, Martha E.: *Planning Our Town,* 1964; *Pockets of Hope,* 1967; *Block by Block,* 1973; New York: Alfred A. Knopf.

National Committee on Urban Growth Policy: *The New City.* New York: Praeger; 1969.

Osborn, Frederic J.: *Green-Belt Cities.* New York: Schoken Books; 1969. With Arnold Whittick: *The New Towns: The Answer to Megalopolis.* Cambridge, Mass.: MIT Press; 1969.

Schaffer, Frank: *The New Town Story.* London: MacGibbon and Kee; 1970.

Stein, Clarence: *Toward New Towns for America.* Cambridge, Mass.: MIT Press; 1966.

Warner, Sam Bass: *Planning for a Nation of Cities.* Cambridge, Mass.: MIT Press; 1966.

# Index

## About the Authors

For many years Martha Munzer has successfully combined her work in science and conservation with her interest in young people. She was among the first women graduates of MIT, and subsequently taught chemistry at the Fieldston School in New York for twenty-five years. Following this she joined the Conservation Foundation where she was a staff member for fourteen years. She then lectured and worked with young people at the Wave Hill Center for Environmental Studies. Martha Munzer has written a number of books for Knopf including *Planning Our Town* and *Block by Block: Rebuilding City Neighborhoods.*

John Vogel Jr. graduated from Carleton College in Minnesota, where he was Phi Beta Kappa. He received a Master's degree in English from the University of Virginia, and also spent a year studying at the University of Lancaster in England.